October,
Michael Lobby

Habitat of Home

Copyright © 2017 by Zephram de Colebi

Cover paintings and illustrations by the author

Cover and interior design by Jean Zeb de la Graves

ISBN 978-1544028415

All rights reserved. No part of this publication may be reproduced, stored in a retrieval system or transmitted in any form or by any means, electronic, mechanical, photocopying, recording or otherwise without prior permission in writing from The Hermitage.
Brief exerpts (fewer than 200 words) are permitted for book reviews in any mechanical or electronic format without prior permission.

Set in 10.5 point Palatino Linotype

Printed in the United States of America by CreateSpace

Published by The Hermitage
75 Grove Road
Pitman, Pennsylvania
United States of America
www.attheHermitage.org

Habitat of Home

The Hoards of Excellence

This is the whole of all a life,
The hoards of excellence,
The velvets of our rooms
Of day, the load we hoarded by.

This is the form of mansioned things,
The hope spun into worlds,
This, culmination of the longing
To be whole, is spelled.

The dames of ancient here,
The shoes of pearl, the home,
The knowing of the greatness,
Rising on a page.

This is the universe, strung,
A moment at each word,
And all else becomes a copy
Of the manuscript, already done.

(1981)

The Habitat of Home

Come taste the bed of orient,
Come touch the beds of pearl,
The brave simplicity of verse,
The habitat of home.

The joyous band of this still spot,
So far from that you know,
I plod to reach that furtherest boundary,
That place of crooked rhyme.

And stroke of fresh philosophy,
Some bold illusion bound,
For poet in his hooded fashion
To breach sublime,

And breathe some momentary thing,
To masses, come to join
The mournful, plodding pages,
Of sobriety refined.

(1985)

Towards Home

I lean towards home,
That chrome sparkled star
In some dusky firmament,
Where no lens discern its silent arc.

I am, as compasses turn north,
From some invisible attraction, magnetized,
As if it were some steady place,
Some land discerned upon some hill,

Some habitat, just rounding at a graceful bend,
Where ageless, child familiar forms
Await like spectral memory
Of welcome, of belonging,

In a constant noon of summer light,
I am about to turn upon the sight,
To shed the heavy, cold unease,
Like skin, formed from foreign places

Where, as stranger for a lifetime
Pushed against dark forms, unyielding
In their alien repulsion
That I had happened to be there.

And grasped at trinkets that reflected
Where I had come from,
My secret belonging place,
I heaped the pictured familiarity

Of things about me, as graven symbols
Of my somewhere haven, of that refuge,
That ancient fireside of comforting,
Of touch that feels like scented breeze.
(2008)

CONTENTS

Introduction	15
1. Self	19
2. Past	199
3. Death	233
4. Love	285
5. Spiritual	365
6. Nature	413
7. Home	439
8. Later Poems	465

INTRODUCTION

This is a collection of a lifetime's work of poetry, created as an act of solitary expression, not for an audience or following. It would have been impossible to write with the expectation and apprehension of a discerning or curious public responding to what was the depth of intimacy for me, a communing with the deepest sense of inspiration, as if written for eyes of the spirit only.

But as is the fate of all artistic endeavor, the finished result takes on a life of its own, and separates itself from the creator. It becomes an artifact of the process of creation, once finished, leaving a product which held such intense passion and foresight into realms that are rarely explored. These poems become the map of a journey, of decades of seeking a connection with the unexpressed, the unknown.

For myself, as unknown as this work, I was born in Damariscotta, Maine, and grew up in Wiscasset, spending two decades there, until embarking on a journey that spread across the entire United States and Canada, to end up living near the small village of Pitman, Pennsylvania, as a reclusive hermit, a Harmonist, living at the Hermitage.

I began my career as a poet at the age of sixteen, as I sat by a dam in the woods near my parents' property, and watched the water cascading down from the spring rains. I had been in the habit of keeping an illustrated journal for some time, and often carried paper with me to write, but had never considered verse for an expression of what I observed about me.

I had been enchanted with the rhymes in an old book we had at home, the complete Mother Goose, and often altered bits of verse to create a form of story telling similar to what was in the book, but had never delved into a form of original creation until that day by the dam. It seemed as if that type of expression came upon me as an evolutionary outpouring of communication, a second language in which I could converse, to create a written documentation of feelings that could not be expressed in any other way.

They were simple, short lines, in which the language could be altered into a cadence, like music, the sound of the words being my notes. I have, over the years, searched for that balance of cadence in my poetry, to give it a chanting effect.

Once begun, I wrote incessantly, two, four, eight line verses, channeling unexpressed emotion into a form which gave me such a release of feeling. What wasn't simple and effortless was the ability to connect with the unknown and write coherently what was within, lying in a state of unformed, raw urges. Coming back to reread certain passages, I found that the release I felt at the time of writing did not translate into anything comprehensible once set alone on the page. The story wasn't forming clearly into words because it was blocked by feelings I had while writing. It was only after the emotion died away, and I could distance myself from an event, or observation, that I could return to it as an artist, and craft a previously unexpressible urge into a clear format.

At many instances, the poems seemed to write themselves, and I would pause, then complete lines as if they had already been formed in my mind. I relized that I had been forming the poem on an unconscious level for some time, until I could write. Even years later a phrase or wording could be clarified, giving it a more refined touch.

My poetry coinsided with artwork, line drawings which would be inked in. Both means of expression formed and grew together, so I have included illustrations to go along with my poems in this book. Drawing and writing were things I could carry with me in my travels and could be produced almost without cost.

Although I wrote poetry for myself, and made little effort to have it published and shared, I have found, now that my efforts in oil painting have taken over almost all of my creative energy, that I owed a debt to the poems themselves to be preserved for their own sake. My personal involvement lessens, and becomes extinct with my death, but the poems continue unchanging, and I have always depended upon the unchanging, the unknown creative force to guide these poems to become a clear expression of that force. They deserve to be preserved for their own sake, and the effect they may have on others.

All of my early artwork and journals were destroyed, and most of my early poems. I led a precarious existence in my early life, and was unable to protect them from the people around me. This body of my work still survives and I feel a great fortune to be able to save them, and bring them to light. They have allowed me to live all these years, and to feel a guiding strength in something that has always sustained me in the midst of uncertainty and change.

At Poetry

Rise now, bloodless specters of delight,
Your fleshy forms no longer abound,
Your warmth decayed to lifeless chill,
Your particle of being, past earthly care.

Rise up, you, my faded paramours,
My sweet embracing shadowed family,
Who are bound to me in aiery death,
As you were, so solidly, in life.

I am your destiny of eternity,
Your final paramour, last love,
Who in this faded twilight of being
Reach to you, a final embrace.

You were my rays of sun in terror forest,
Steady compass in unknown dark,
My rainbow'd delight in solitary stillness,
Children of my being, masters of my breath.

So we are joined upon this nuptual pyre,
As flames consume our room of day,
Char into oblivion our watchful pose,
Consume what we had been, to ash.

Yet phoenix'd bound, you rise
As sparks into the firmament,
Expose to worldly journeyers
Your once all solitary being, now awake.

(2017)

1. Self

So Soon Forget

So soon forget the prison camp
We lived in, barely live,
With shackles for our diadems,
And damp for soft, and stench for air.

When saved a year ago,
Can safely lift our straightened spine,
Alike the ones who never bent,
Go unnoticed now, almost akin.

So now uncomfortable with slight,
When not too long ago we welcomed pain,
That showed we could still feel,
And proved we were alive.

Yet not too deep we really laugh,
In these societies,
Where subjects live on want, and we, in need,
When every fruit we touch,
Could soon remind us of a barren tree.

We dare not kiss too long some lip,
For fear it will not be the same,
And change without us,
Towards some goal we cannot reach,
Our symptoms still remain.

Though what the cause, is less in view,
And we become spontaneous,
Survivors of the wreck, on land at last,
You never would have thought
Had ever been to sea.

(1973)

So Late We Build

So late we build, and yet so soon despise
The hard worked magic now at our side,
Smelted from some mountain, hardest to climb,
And took dear cost
We would have sold the world to keep.

But build we do, though reason dim
Lies fainted in some moss grown Tomb,
And its still memory, once alive, we build upon,
Foundations less seen than sought, to hold.

Life comes shorter than its meaning,
And we must go anon,
Past scraping expectations lifted high,
That make so little suitable for holding long.

Away from strength we move,
The stifled house abandoned, shriek
Its silent decay, that we could little stop,
And leaves a ruin,
To deplete the burdened ground.

(1975)

Work the Tattings Wait

I strive upon the sitting room,
To mingle with the elders, gone to dust,
And take my place at clock, and chair,
And work the tattings wait,
At fingers to perfection skilled
With needles, and a silken thread,
And turn my passions, stitch by thought
Into the safety there,
Where change is only to a silence,
And danger, less than memory.

(1975)

My Windowless Estate

In my windowless estate, there are angels here,
Who crawl amid the dust, their molted wings
Scraping in the dark, like wounded animals,
Dragging numb limbs past the accident,
Or hunter's sharp response.

I hear them bump round ancient things,
In endless search for particle of light, I would assume,
Though I could tell them that the walls
Go thick forever.

And there is no hope to change the dark,
There are no locks to fit the keys
We may have had, some lit flashed day,
Upon a slope of greenwood, when at child.

Dull and Sober now, the broad estate,
Adult circumference surround, surprising in its eternity,
It last so long, and we so still,
To hear the fragments shake themselves,
Almost at peace.

Though I dare not move to stir the dark,
Some horror in it wait, I think,
To turn this silent night to flames,
And scorch me with hot sulfur in the sitting room.

The Hunter in the City

The hunter in the city, out of bounds,
Soon exchanges in his need,
Some inner stalking now, forest of nerve

Where he goes deep into the hideaways,
And shoot pain bullets in the thick,
And clay marked bogs of specters,
Haunting where he step.

And you would never know he was a man
Of bounding plaid, and smelled of autumns,
And coffee ground, now in his city,
Deep in pavement loss.

Just thinking to survive the only way he can,
His gun rust dusted in some ruin shop,
His coats so out of shape,
And nowhere to extend his stride.

He seems like any vision in the noise,
Where we for any fortune would invest
His nature wrapt around us, but we finally wrap him
In our hunted hold.

(1976)

The Weight

The weight seems almost done at times,
Our shoulder almost strong,
A moment to release a sorrow
Into quietness.

To lay its wearied head away,
To straighten all its limbs,
And say a funeral prayer to heaven,
And put it in the ground.

And go to sleep after the pain,
As if a fainted child,
Until a knock into the brain, come
Almost unheard, like snow,

Descend upon us like a thought.
And then our breathing stops to wait,
Until we answer what the noise could be,
And we turn to the thing,

And let the being in,
And stiffen as it climbs upon us,
Like an ancient man whose crippled shape
Remains, from sightless burdens that he wore.

(1978)

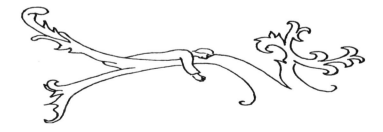

There is a Sound

There is a sound the soul makes
When it is unwound,
Like springs of clocks when they are tightened
Past their boundary of tight.

And ever then the tick is out,
Like some gigantic shadow left,
And all the gears are forfeited
To silence, at a pause.

The form seem same,
There is no notice at the glass,
Of what has done within,
Except the quieting.

And like us, just a lack of sound,
Tells all the soul has been,
And with it, we will never know the magnitude
Of loss, until our gauges run again.

When I no Longer Feel

When I no longer feel the words,
When I no longer see,
There comes a fading of the tick,
The drifting of sobriety,

No longer bound at sense.
It is a letting go of courtly expectation.
Since we are not the king,
No one will notice if we turn away

And seek that click upon the brain.
That can be all we know of peace,
A conscious sleeping, insulated from
The nagging voices droning, as a hive.

The active expectations gone, the yoke
Slipped just an inch, so we may
Rub the swollen shoulder marks,
That never have grown numb.

But escape is just a summer early dream,
Blurring the prison room,
Some caged beast pacing slowly, but not
Feeling the wire mesh which guides his step.

(1996)

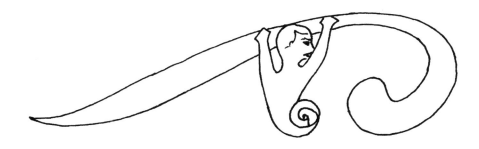

We Were Helpless Once

Mama, why did you let me be?
Too many babies sittin' in a tree,
Didn't have room for you and me.
Why did you let him beat me all day?
There just wasn't anything I could say.
Why did you let him tear at my clothes?
I don't remember, no one knows.
Why did you let him tear at my dick?
The thought of it still makes me sick.
It ruined me for making love.
The helplessness like stars above,
Formed a constellation in my brain,
That late of night I still call pain.
And all the chances there could be
For tenderness, or closeness, or intimacy,
All died that afternoon, you see.
And you watched him do this cruelest thing,
And still, at making supper, you would sing.
I don't remember, it was just a day.
Let so long ago now pass away.
He turned the channel of my fate,
And not remembering, is far too late,
Because the wound could never heal.
My haunted son, it's no big deal,
You'll never know the things I feel.
The things he did to me, as well,
To make me heartless, who can tell
What could have been?
I loved you once, I loved you then.
I cannot tell you all the things
That made me what I am, to sing,
To sing in terror, what could I do,
For he destroyed the joy, in me, and you.

(1999)

The Gods Sleep On

The gods sleep on because they cannot die,
Across the marble benches,
Have worn the golden goblets out
Which once held pleasure, mixed with pain.

And nothing stirs their mighty brows,
For all the words and possibilities
Have been experienced,
And warm sensation pales to numbing cold.

But child's prayers still mumble up to them
From ruined temple ground,
Their last all faithful followers,
Still make a joyous sound.

"Gonna go to heaven in a hickory boat,
Sing and dance all evening
If she stays afloat,
In my brand new body, never miss a note.

"I like to lie and think to die,
My tongue stuck to my throat,
And go to glory, cold and gory,
Upon a snow white goat.

"Ashes, ashes, thrown in grasses,
Spill into the water,
Where the bones of Mama crashes,
Gives you great big gashes.

"Rock a bye my baby boy,
You were not good enough to be my joy,
And daddy never went a hunting,
And baby never had his bunting,
And never wrapped his baby in."

(1999)

Son's Song

I can't get my baggage through
Your door, Mama, maybe next
Year I will try again,
But you have piled so much against the door.

It becomes so hard to find you,
And I hate your resignation to me,
Like a homely face in a mirror,
You see yourself, and cannot love

The image. The flat reflection
Never lets you see, or touch,
Or feel the warm flesh,
Or know there is a princess behind the glass.

Why did you keep your arms
So tightly folded like a Shaker dance,
So stiff, when I was so soft,
And needed those iron bands to hold me in?

To shape me for the outlands, where
I would be thrown so soon,
And only skills of solitude to bring,
You never looked, or waved goodbye

As I stood there on the city street,
Alone in ways I was to learn
The great, infested city would only deepen.
And to survive,

Must be so shallow, and thin,
To slip unnoticed in the roar,
That did not touch, like fog,
Yet made me turn invisible.

(1999)

Yes

Last love, sweetest, best love,
Let us remake ourselves together.
You, in your raw prime brotherhood
Needing daily kissing down.

Like licking down spent horses, panting,
Having run, are honey musk warm,
And wet,
And I have them in my mouth.

And it is you I call the words,
And you I dream to waken to,
Having been so long away,
To come back to feel at male,

Whose skin perspires in me,
And draws me back in to him,
Like home, he is fit just right,
I want to stuff down in my throat.

(2000)

Lover of a God

I am lover of a god you cannot see,
Who pushes away the need in me,
Who spends the hours locked away,
Hiding where he cannot be

Kissed until his body heats,
And tongue down in his nakedness,
Until he would moan an honest prayer
In me.

He will not let divinity be free,
He will not be the thing he needs to be,
How has it become the nature
Of the young to be so old?

Supple beauty cold,
His slushy hugs would dampen me,
But my heat is bold,
Of furnaces on Vulcan's Forge,

Where I have drossed out
Slag heaps by the century
Until he came,
I stepped through flame into this sea.

I did not lessen in the hiss,
Like ancient gods no more believed,
I wait, unable to dissolve,
Am stark, and still.

(2000)

A Final Room

What home is here, a final room,
Low ceilings overhead,
Small windows clouded,
In this narrow space.

It is a place the aged know,
Who were born some century ago,
It is a place the weary go,
Muffling their voice.

A place of solitary still,
A place along no road,
A place past reach of touching,
We lean into despite our will.

The Quiet Man

It is the constant wind that moves, not selves,
It is external forces that blow,
While selves remain in place.

The endless blast outside the door,
Numbs senses by its ferocity
To roar around us, while we are still.

In some cabin built upon a wilderness,
We have come to, for search of treasure
That has not been taken for the land is hard,

And does not yield to careless speculation of the site,
It does not attract the weak,
Who move endlessly with their goals.

Brute men, who are too thick to feel this wind,
Brunt on by it, while the quiet man
Extends into it, and becomes the air.

(2000)

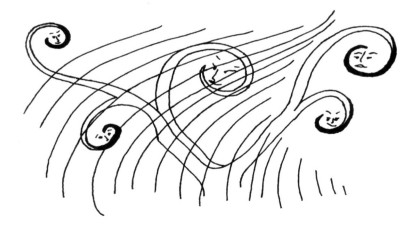

The Standard for our Being

The standard for our being, mold
Around us as a thing,
Some hem extended in a velvet,
Some room where grandsires sit,

Remind us of the boundary of self,
In each article, each, a momentary check
Of what the human is,
Against the vastness of a wilderness.

We carve the shape that speak ourselves,
As if some solidarity in form
Take on the judgment to our being,
And we condition to the room.

Select our station, in material,
And gird the oaken planks amid the floor,
As temple ground, in plaster holiness,
Strive barely to acquire consciousness.

Je Me Souviens

I remember when I said I wanted to sleep alone,
And how you said nothing.
Hot boy, fire in your pants boy,
No more sex for you boy.

I lived with you through your smooth face,
Now lined, but the insides stayed smooth.
How could you get any now, boy,
When everyone said no, even in the best of times.

And I always found touch a mistake,
Because I never felt touched inside,
Never felt beautiful, inside,
Although the men were beautiful.

Raw men, I wanted someone.
Somewhere genes and consciousness conflicted,
What I needed and wanted and got, never matched,
Then there was you,

Who bound to me in grim determination, to create,
To be everything, despite the pull of convention,
The thick minded, nothing people,
Whose only act, seemed to be attacking us.

You can smell someone different,
And all that hardship drew me away from you,
These nights alone, it seems I am on the edge
Of silence, not feeling outside,

Never having meant to be so isolated from you,
But the intimacy we clung to was the one thing
I could not pose, and pretend with,
And my nakedness grew to feel
Like a thing with its shell torn off.

(2000)

Cool Sun

The isolation cools us,
And we cannot compare it to a thing,
Or remove it for speculation,
Or join it to a better thing.

It is the one cool sun
That illuminates even light,
Enhances brightness, yet we do not shield ourselves,
Because it does not burn the eyes.

(2000)

The Distraction of Light

It is an outward sign of inner clarity
That does not sway to custom,
Does not build thorn towers,
Dripping ice bitch queen venom for control of everything.

It is the sign of quest few can know.
The lonely trail, which in itself is life,
Its movement quiet and slow because it is not warm,
It does not follow moths to glow.

It does not dip in nature's heat,
Supple male forms cannot detract it,
Only shadow where it is relieved from view,
To see, or be seen, without the distraction of light.

We Wait

We wait, for nothing that we can think of,
No memory, or hope, or longing to be else,
Or, for some souvenir to rise and take us
To that once ago.

Because of just a nothing left to do,
From all the boundaries of space,
The solitary remnant that remain, is still,
And having sunken to the spot, we are,

Now antiquated in a drawer, some heavy frame
Close on us, as a dark, and we are still,
No longer midst activity,
Some faded curiosity to the outer world,
Which turns us slowly out of style.

There is an ache - 1

There is an ache too wide for form,
I press against at time,
As if diminishing myself, or enlarging,
Just to see the scope of it.

And stiffen, as the inability to move from such unease
Spark all desire to comprehend the thing,
Which is still suffered, suddenly,
As I am still confronting it.

Its childhood, formlike memory,
A lifetime then, I pass each moment
Like a volume into me,
And wonder how to have experienced

Such vivid lines into the brain,
Where since a time, shut down
That vast ability,
And have not felt another way since then.

There is an ache - 2

There is an ache too wide for form,
I press against, at time,
As if diminishing myself, or expanding,
To see just the scope of it.

And stiffen, as the inability to move,
Make all desire to be from the thing,
You would not know I descended from that place,
As foreign as I am, confronting it.

Its childhood, formlike memory,
A lifetime then, I pass each moment
Like a volume, into me,
And wonder how to have experienced

Such vivid images into the brain,
Where since a time shut down
That vast ability,
And have not felt another way since then.

The Silent Words

The silent words repeat till we are dumb,
The never having said things,
That are left alive, as if they were the boldest
Actions that have been.

Just the silence speak, as if it had not gone
To rest, so many centuries
Of past departed from, without a souvenir,
And all laid final in.

The places are not like they were,
Evolved, themselves, amid some secret destiny,
Who would have thought more than a setting
For our own resolve.

And now we are some different, than ago,
Bound straightward in our trap of fate,
Unnoticing the newer possibilities of quieting,
Being mired in our share
Of could have been.

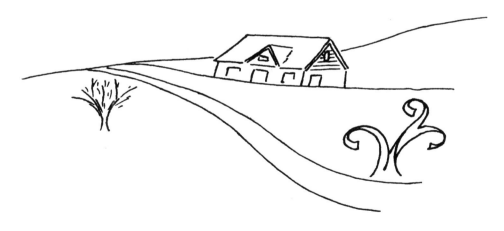

The Light

It was the light, then I
Had felt awakening, to come,
As Lazarus, who must, some similar,
Have felt himself return to sun,

And day, who once more in the warm,
Let sharp, revealing light return,
And be exposed, and once more,
Come to senses, like a school bell calls.

To place us in sobriety,
And join the stationed figures,
Rising like ourselves,
Who rush to beat the day clock,
To our morning pose.

Toward that Once

There is a spot I can recall,
As if all being since then had grown,
And none before, and I came somehow,
Lessening, while all the world expand.

This happening I could not tell you,
No fortune recreate the incident
At shattering, we are not built on senses
That record destructions of a kind

That are invisible, and yet unto the place
I linger, as a compass,
Pointing, toward that once,
When all of me was magnetized.

What has Been

As if some creature then, where we were, ago,
Had begun its life,
And grew into us, as a child,
Then man, who served, and dressed us,

And became familiar as the mansion ground
That all defined our self.
And what had lingered
Was our reality, sweet the filtered light,

There upon the worn things
Hands and feet had touched,
That are no more.
Their memory was still upon the stair,

Their life within the drawers.
That creature was the bedrock being,
There are still traces of,
If you were to examine what has been.

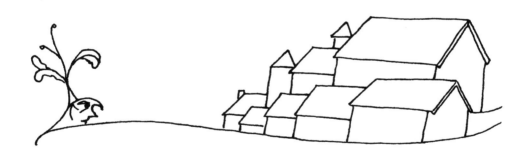

There is a House

There is a house within the self,
We hear of quietly,
It is not larger than the whole of us,
And easy to be in.

Where we are never older than a memory
Requires, and the job of the inhabitants
As simple as a thread they pull
Upon the hope of wait.

And though the vehicle of life put out,
The house remain in all its things,
To shake down at the present, to some
Later inhabitant, who find a strange familiarity.

The Value of a Self

The value of a self, is silence,
Earned unnoticed at the blare
Of consciousness, as its owners use
To pry their being into the form

Some sire stipulated was necessity
To bind the urging instincts
Into trinket, easy worn,
And borne as standard, louding, everywhere.

The Source of Needing

The source to needing is often undiscovered.
Its presence made in observation
Of not having just the thing,
We cannot place as object, or as time.

An urge among the instinct,
To be satisfied, its symbols are for sale
As souvenir of family, or some extinguished
Elegance, needed to be owned.

As if their own discovery,
Somehow created just the familiarity to them,
As if some ancient self,
Came visible through tinted photograph.

And since then, ever stood,
Some longing to be closer
To the speechless pull, that
Offers greater emptiness with gain.

In View Of

First what we liked, not, the best,
Then, what we must have, two, of,
Next, comes what we'll do, without,
In, view of.

(1968)

At Being Child

I mourn, forever, every, day,
As if at being Child,
Everyone had grown their fullest,
And I, immortal, stay.

Being less, and low, and Dull,
Ashamed of nook, or Tree,
Frightened, at the common land,
Now Ugly singularity.

And posted with the News, of Great,
How Conquerors, have been,
And Wonder how they study magic,
And how the Worlds, are small.

And Creep in Anguish, anywhere,
And bolt the Daylight out,
Try to reason, with a Ruin,
And find it in Myself.

I Call Upon the Skies

I call upon the Skies which move of air,
For just a halting breath,
And put my simple gift in dungeons
For fear it is not mine to hold.

And guard the way, and watch the thing,
Its wings as leaves, so drop,
And coil upon the floor in Silence,
And lie there, still.

So, childless, I leave the castle stone,
And turn myself away,
To beg the sky again for something,
Upon me, lay.

(1973)

Payment for Myself

I am frugal to the brink of fear,
Though not of some necessity,
Nor chosen, but in some state of destiny,
Of winters in a flake, where blizzard blow.

I sit in my still cabin, silent,
No dare to move, lest passion break
Upon nothing, and I depositor of its rotted head,
Am burdened down again.

What sense of rage, an ounce of sound
Would glut me in its hold, with hollow walls,
And none to hear, and cold, to make the
Booming voice so sharp, it almost penetrate itself.

Less, and less, until on air I spend too much,
And very space, extravagant, and could I
Disappear from nothing, and squeeze the words,
It might be just a payment for myself.

The Thing

To hide as if a changeling babe,
To guilty mother in the light,
Who clutches as if it might grow worldly,
And show her truer self.

We must be gentle, with the thing,
As if it were an ether around us,
Breathe in silence, fainting
At joy that we withstand.

Of Lesser Battles

Though war be done, who has not won,
Adjust his sword anew,
For other lesser battles, not of king,
Or fortress stone.

But some unyielding, future thing,
He ready at the call,
To challenge inner skirmishes,
To fight invisibles.

The Sound Within

The sound within the brain, forewarn
A rising of the thing,
Known by its shapeless figuration,
Pressing into form.

As some collected monster, bound,
Its several heads unwind,
Toward scraping in the skull,
For some escape, into the air,

Yet, seem to satisfy itself,
After a while, move still,
Pausing in the tortured mind,
Now bending to contain it in.

And then, as if a fire come,
Its heat in wave-like move,
Motion rage into the consciousness,
Until it bloat, like numb.

The Inner Place

The inner place we call the heart,
Bleeds loneliness when it pulses quietly
Past the senses, like some crack down in the brain,
No synapse know.

And who can pry it when at such longing,
The solace that comes so plentiful
In daily activity, will not staunch,
We feel a superficial comforting.

Except at memory, that safe, unburdened place,
Her old light calms, as we were happy then,
That once ago, in some moment
That still presses in, though the form went out,

Some century. We linger at the tender thing,
As if it was a mother, now gone to dust,
Our need as like some lost child reaching
For the bunting of that safest place,

That keep it like a universe within,
And all the particles relax,
And time fade ancient like some pendulum
That stopped in us, and kept the need in gear.

Where Seasons Stop

Here is the place where seasons stop,
Here the sediment of memory, grow still,
And we are clear,
As if departed from the world we knew.

Or lone survivor of some forgotten thing,
Not having souvenir of what we were,
We linger in the foreign land,
Of city animal, who prowls its pathways fearlessly.

And to this land of alien,
We only know what we are not,
And learn the habits of the beasts,
And watch them from our room, or cell.

Where We Have Come From

Ages where we have come from,
Our heritage, our fate,
As if atoms, on some star illuminated,
Or some depth of ocean sunk

Upon some beast, whose air is dark,
And all within, a silence,
Like some heaviness,
We are that dust, that once ago.

We do not comfort in just being live,
It seems the world has always been,
And we, it seems for us, the ages were
Completing for our judgment, and dispose.

And we are mired, with the mass,
Normality of dull consciousness abound,
Until those moments of removal or despair,
We clutch a god, or family, for worth.

Some Remembrance Amid the Whir

Like some remembrance amid the whir,
There came a sound, you do not sense,
Like dog pitch, lingering in silence,
That only synapse know.

Yet jolts to permanence, into the form,
Like worlds exploded at the thing,
And left it charred forever,
With the noticeless extreme.

As if some pixie, crushed afoot,
As if a castle burned,
Because we touched unknowingly,
And caused us with its fate.

Some unexpected, fatal reach,
And to the sightless curse,
We lie, as if ingested fury's agony,
And squirm unconsciously.

What Forms Deem

To what culture's forms deem insanity,
We are finally outed, to display
At last our colors of the reckoning
Of this so secret posing, now exposed.

To mumble fair words incoherently
To specters round us, lilting
In faint shadows of this final destiny
We lean into, like home, having remembered strength,

To fuel us from internal sources.
It is not with regret we remain here,
The new land is spare, yet rich
In imagination of our separateness

Of solitary work, that externals fear.
For we, not dependents of those
Who have adopted rules of their behavior
To unite in cold repetition of endless conformity,

Are survivors, denied even common air,
Shunned, now without restraint,
Left in what faint existence we can glean,
From when we were adaptable.

Are free now, to sift this blackened paradise
In rags, stiff hair streaming out,
Wild eyes widening that are turned within,
Have finally come out.

Reversed, what was so hidden, now our shape,
What was our longing, now our selves,
Like organs, our hidden, secret sanity,
Lies sealed like Pharaoh's golden tombs.

(2002)

The Distant Area of Now

There is a silence that I know,
To mark the place I have been from,
Its memory, a stiffening along the brain,
As if some danger zone.

Some helpless place I stood in once,
Soft, unformed by bone,
And was pressed into a shell
That formed new presence of myself.

I feel the shape, am rounded by the thing,
Its early crush, bound, lingering,
Upon the distant area of now,
I cover with a veil.

And cripple into light, my movement,
Halting step, with half a likeness on,
And wonder at the could have been,
Whole, might have guided me to be.

Do Not Remember

Do not remember, old thing.
That place is far from us,
And we no longer share hopes,
Having been from everywhere,

And cast off like used things.
Only that was too long ago,
Our room has grown antique in waiting,
And we would find a different greeting,

Should we return to that society.
We have become the thing that they desire most,
Genuine in workmanship, of quality
That only improves by being left alone.

We would not recognize the faces there,
That would press upon us.
Taking now, our hard earned value,
To ease their cheapness.

Let us stay, here, bound into each other,
Entwined in arms that never tire.
So sealed is our hidden spot,
That time pauses, to relieve us of futures,

And worthless pasts.
It is not us that lived then,
Not altered, to this place of quiet,
We are just wind that moans beyond the glass.

(2002)

This is Not The Place

This is not the place we have been from.
Though silent, not stillness in hiding
To protect ourselves, not waiting,
For that is a thing to do with hope.

It is a better place, secret, past finding,
For to be here is some form of destiny
Travelers cannot gain, nor experience,
Navigate the finding of its view.

Here, that quality of word is all survivors know,
Who wake no longer victim of their wreck.
To be, as if they had been always
Placed away from what is known as world.

To be familiar with this station, land
Of finished things, where comfort finally
Enwraps scarred shoulders, not hiding,
Not holding in, not even memory sustains.

(2002)

Here The Rooms Are Spread - 1

We are dressed, the light is passed,
And here the rooms are spread
With ancient things, familiar in their place,
Have remained, no more in use.

It is a station we have assumed
In these late hours, sentinel over soft decay,
That always seemed our destiny,
Always apart when we were close

To flesh, lain sleeping by us.
Who could have known we were the thing
That pleasures could not hold,
No matter how they warmed us

In that deep heat. We were too old
To be so young, the touch had died
In fists, when we were helpless once.

And take our weathered place, not broken,
Not a mourning for some other place,
It is in the stillness like a monument,
We wear our homemade princess gown
For nothing but a memory of our fairyland selves.

(2002)

Here the Rooms are Spread - 2

We are dressed, the light is passed,
And here the rooms are spread
With ancient things, familiar in their place
Have remained, no more in use.

It is a station we have assumed
In these late hours, sentinel over soft decay
That always seemed our destiny,
Always apart when we were close

To flesh, lain sleeping by us.
Who could have known we were the thing
That pleasures could not hold
No matter how they warmed us

In that deep heat. We were too old
To be so young, the touch had died
In fists when we were helpless once.

And take our weathered place, not broken,
Not a mourning for some other place,
It is the stillness like a monument,
We wear our homemade gown
For nothing but a memory of ourselves.

(2002)

New Anatomy

Some twinge clapped silently, as if inside
Marked new anatomy, and I was filled with tiny parts
That worked in spools and belts,
And something had gone wrong amid the whir.

Some useful section in the tatted brain
Now raveled, and a disc had bent beneath my chest,
And mild on my exterior, a shudder of the news
That my machinery had failed.

Slight the loss, no ear so close enough to tell
My tick is out of time, and I am damaged
Like a crack in crystal destined to a shelf,
To hide its ruined flaw.

And seem abright to passing fanciers,
I stand just out of touch,
And linger, thoughtful of the moment
When I felt the change,
And stepped into forever, with a weakness on.

(1975)

Incidental

A loss no greater than a Day,
A thought as steep as ease,
How incidental, are the lot
That rest upon themselves.

(1971)

The Careless Stars

That I may rise beyond, is dull,
As if I had just been,
And do not, think of all the places,
Where to be, would glorify.

To remain, is cautious thing,
As others are away,
And place is of its own, perfection,
And cares not what I do.

The day is dim, and as a night,
Contents itself to be,
To stand as holder of the network,
That holds the careless stars.

The Beast

The Beast wonders, at the world,
And how it Breeds its spawn,
And how so tiny, grow the frailest,
Who have a kingdom to put on.

And bear the worldly greater need,
And bind in terror, high,
So go the half Gods spun in Magic,
With simple mothers' soul.

(1971)

Missive Inkiness

Prisoner of page, am I,
Of missive Inkiness,
The power children Bursting lightly
To Solitude of Life.

Who deadly are, that do not breathe,
And tomblike semblance,
But I think a vast perfection,
To be so silent cast.

(1973)

Magistrates

It is not safe, to be at Home,
When Magistrates are poor,
And used to eat of dew, and air,
And now seek higher things.

They smile, as we invite them in,
And notice every wall,
As if by incident, grow jolly,
And ask us what we do.

And turn, and move us round, to see,
And grasp our faces tight,
And squeeze, and hold us like an object,
They would like to eat, or be.

(1973)

Myself

I used to wish upon myself,
I used to never Dream,
And found it royal in the Season,
That continue everywhere.

And used to worship Gods, and thing,
Upon my land, and place,
And found it unified, and holy,
And ever in Grace.

And spun in flower, and Pearl,
And loved the Wind, and sea,
And captured shells I put Upon me,
As if infinity.

(continued)
And sped into my Soul, the news,
That perfect was the place,
And I was great, and great was with Me,
In earthen faith.

And ageless was it there, and still,
And moonbeams chose their Nests, and resting,
Lit diamond everywhere,
That I gathered by the Shore,

And died, how little to be Known,
When suddenly at Breath,
The ether touch her Lip with finger,
And shake her head, no More.

Then I am in my Tomb, of stone,
And find the walls to Breathe,
And put them in my lungs, and lie,
And grow accustomed to the dark.

And Maybe centuries, it Was,
And maybe never time, have lain,
To hear the ocean, in its fancy,
And I, in lifeless pain.

Forgetting all, more Slowly now,
Are more afraid to Go than stay,
For fear I just imagined, being,
Or fear it just imagined me.
(1973)

Without My Crown

Without my crown I had forgotten Royalty,
And guessed their invitations, out of date,
Some kind, though uncommitted thought,
Of What had been,
And I no gown quite suitable, for their Society.

Though I had once been greatest, with the best,
And shone my finest stars, with all their Light,
For earth, and planets to be Governed by,
And comforted, that they stood Stable
With such majesty.

All I can Remember, I was satisfied,
And eternity just room, being pleasant, in,
And freedom was a golden chain we loved to Spin,
To snare each lonely soul, with delight.

I can almost think of where I, used to Be,
And just see glory coming on a Plain,
And feel an ancient touch,
From Gods that must have been,
But sink still lower with this Weight of now
On so unsolid ground.

It Was as If

It was as if the world had stilled,
And I kept spinning, burst around it,
Through forests and ocean, ever Turning
Upon some old axis, now out of style.

This new earth, dim and in some silence,
As if at Babe, I scanned its groping form,
And life was out of time, this second land,
Dying in its novice breath, a newborn stench.

And I awoke, to find it True,
From dreams, the limitless expanse,
Encircling my head in crowns of wire,
And eyes, opening my open eyes, to all see all.

And I am still upon the land,
So unfamiliar, with my packs of dew and Web,
This stone land, with my winds of Ether,
That buffet me along the craggy Granite zone.

(1973)

So Little Great

So little great, that would I breathe,
The earth would moan a loss,
And I be wracked for payment for its due,
And would but beg, had I the room.

So tighten in my little form, in shadow go,
For fear I could not pay the light,
So empty that I cannot move,
Lest move cry out that I am here,
And cannot give.

Quality of Gem

The quality of Gem,
Refuse a second hand,
And Royalty put out of season,
Grow worn in soft demise.

The stooping lad, brought out of will,
Has perished lowest out,
A memory of stone, and worship,
A faultless insufficiency.

(1974)

Methods of Our Mode

I bathe him in the tunney lilts
Prepared of ether, down,
Measureless, unique, and royal,
Simplifying balm.

Methods of our mode,
Glomerate of glee,
Stationed to containing ever,
Lackless conditioning.

(1974)

Moment

Moment is a loss of sight,
Through noticing it by,
Century, to hungry owners
Squandering their find,

Particle of fortitude,
The trinket fellowship,
Possessor of the universes,
Tiniest of beat.

Girder of the instants,
Unable to withhold,
Showing to the world, producing,
Scenes of reverie.

Binding motion, following,
Patterns, unity,
Helpless is the chain of ever,
Continuing eternity.

(1974)

The Dreams of Shalimar

I am broken past the dark of never light,
And carry rotting children in the still,
Their bloated faces bumping by the wet-soft trees,
As I go deepest in the forest of despair.

No hope for them, the earth is full,
No place to put the children down in peace,
I must be yet their only messenger of care,
To carry on this journey of eternity.

Cry for us, oh dismal stones,
There are no other faces in the gloom to call,
And you may soon as weep, as they may live,
And I prepare to rest in scope of light.

(1974)

Spices All Have I

Spices all have I, to give,
In casks of Zanzibar,
In frigates round the sea,
To tempt and lavish at a wish.

Though still the barges lie, at flat waves,
No one having made a pledge
To give them course and cargo destiny,
Though small, would never overlook,
And biggest not too roomy to be lost.

Except, I cannot pry an ounce,
Myself alone, at fortune, with a trunk of crowns,
That once held continents by majesty,
And now are burden to put on,
Without the court and circumstance.

(1974)

On the Other Side

On the other side of Day,
I clear my eyes and lie,
Come through now, tarnished with scar and rope,
So I could scarce have thought to breathe

This new air, crisp, and burnished with new intent,
And sun above, and feet below,
And light of golden furnaces abright,
I press new legs upon the polished soil.

To soon abreast expand my joyous stride,
Deep discover this new land, the earth
Of justly toil, deserving rest,
Guilt and grief away.

But till I stand, I will still feel the other land,
Destruction in its waves to knock me down,
And hands still clutching at my rising feet,
And sloth disguised as death, to gird me round.

(1974)

After Our Despair

After our despair, we last,
Somehow survived, internal landscapes littered
With replaceless, broken things,
And we are still as dust inside the air.

As if the violence had rested,
Unbelieving that we had endured,
And sunk, and bled, and moaned,
In fury like the winds.

Like peace out of exhaustion come,
No more as able to contain
A thought of terror, or demise,
And then the forces leave us, to renew.

(1975)

Budded at the Snow

Budded at the snow, I gird
Round spaces in the air
For warmth, I lean upon the thought
Of sun for sustenance,
And vision in the blast some worse,
For faith I may be kept intact.
As difficult as cold to grow,
I bind my failing grasp
Upon the altar ground,
And stand alone in testament
Of life where any cost is paid.

(1975)

The Snowy Petals

I touch the snowy petals of this worn circumstance,
And wonder how they manage in the cold,
So gentle weigh the damage of their heavy stems.
My garden, sparse with tulips matted down,
Still cycling their bulb necessity,
Regardless of the winter, having left its solstice.

(1975)

Each Moment Lost

What is bigger than the day,
Each moment lost, each hour just
Another notice that we've failed,
And sunlight, vision

That we might not miss,
For memory to torture in the dark
With little agonies there was not time for
During light.

What faith, what horror,
To expose the withered lips to food
That they may live,
And suffering have altar for its feast.

(1976)

Helpless Touched

The midnights that I keep awake,
Each, find me silent in their dark,
Awaiting as they pass away,
Some tap, or light, or special sound.

Vigilant in quietness,
Heart my only beat that moment by,
A last religion in this early tomb of life,
A sacrament to bless the hours of my stay,
Or judgment day begun.

I cannot guess the reverence,
Out of loneliness, or doom,
There is no sorrow so collected,
And I so helpless touched.

(1976)

In a Little Town

With pinion needles do I tie,
And sew my soul in form,
And bind into it patterns of the stillness,
And soften it with gauze.

And hook it on me like a gown,
And smooth it round my form,
And wait, the waiting is perfection
In a little town.

(1976)

Like a Breath

As if inside me, like a breath
From some new special thing,
I woke, as different now as quality
Inside a dungeon floor.

As if some homeless seed began
To root me in itself,
And I was kinship now in forests,
And thought in branch-like things.

And felt the movement of the night,
And now my eyes could slit and see,
And I ran ravaging a horror,
In animal extreme.

(1976)

Frozen Substance

Through some inheritance, or fame,
Were I carried to the palace
Of some family name,
And placed there through some fate,

And reconstructed, good of great,
I would no more than now, the plan,
My simple room, and gird my apron
At the day, and strive some little way.

And bind my simple prayers at room,
Dependent of a daffodil, or moment
At the air, or diamond in the snow,
And wear the frozen substance of my crown.

(1976)

Just Resurrected Yesterday

Just resurrected yesterday, I pin my bracelets
Round the shackle scars, and loop my hem
Below the lashes that I almost feel.
I bind the satin at my waist,

And tie each thumb sized pearl into my ragged hair,
And in procession to the masses,
Go in majesty, the queen now stationed at her glory,
To her people stand.

Lost, not long ago, she begged for pain to feel
Some anything, to tell that she was live,
And crawled amid the horrors, that to herself,
Were somehow logic, that at child

She must have too sweetly dreamed
To be so ruined now,
To calculate each loss so well,
And so alone for company, and faith.

Now, and as she reaches all herself come true,
The castle, gilt and golden, with open doors for her,
The perfume balmed forget,
About to comfort in each petal at her feet,

She lingers, while the crowd awaits her to be grand,
And blurs into a dungeon where she step.
This newfound solitude, exchanging pain for numb,
Or ruin for such sorrow

That she felt too deeply to enjoy too long
This chance and whim,
That placed her where few others reach,
Propels her like a graven idol, into this glittered breach.

(1976)

Passion Without Skill

Passion without skill, my will,
That take me into exile,
And out of home, and lingering
Upon some foreign plane.

Fortunes out of range, my scope,
In empty majesties,
Crawling in and out of weakened sustenance,
And turning into mire.

And bitter go the thought of better things,
That are somewhere apart, from me,
And ever on the crest of hillside,
Some hope of mansion burn.

(1976)

Suddenly the Ropes were Pearl

Suddenly the ropes were pearl,
The shackles all a diadem,
And all the weight removed in instants,
All the thorns, a rose.

With just the news that others failed,
And others came this way,
And somehow lost a star of greatness,
That felt a comforting.

That someone choked an earth of screams
And bolted out the light.
And felt in gasps and longing wonder,
And grasped eternity.

And knew the gods, where all they stood,
And worshiped mightily,
To be a moon child, wrapped in splendor,
And silent as a night.

(1976)

Terror Forms

I am of ruin in this state,
Where terror forms may breed
Their bold excesses to the landscape,
Their ugliness abound.

My room of quiet threatened now,
The daying finding out
What particles are hidden from her,
And where to pry the easiest.

The cracks alight, the air in beam
Come to me like a loss,
And deeper down the dungeon going,
I hide where nothing come.

(1976)

Voices Yet Unheard

Someday the voices, yet unheard,
Will organize such sound
The portals of my throat will crumble,
Mouth flail opening.

And scream until the rocks decay,
And universes split,
And world descend to crumble in its sphere,
And age reverse itself.

And fill myself so full of burst
My molecules will spin
Into the being that I linger, till that time,
To cross the void and be.

(1976)

Invisibles of Soft Caress

There is a touch that does not reach,
Invisibles of soft caress,
Drawn movement of desire spun
In threads of silent web.

It is the solitary room,
It is the mind's display,
In looking out from unseen portals
The happenstance of day.

The flesh that form a feast of light,
The movement of a face,
The stretch of sinew, curve of limb,
The warmth of feel within.

The satisfaction of sobriety,
The clarity of chaste delight,
The lingering of sweet enrapture,
Untarnished by the surfeit past the sight.

(2008)

Inner Window, Looking Out

The age reflect its masses mask,
Like Inca gear, its external form
Reflect an inner window looking out,
Slanted, uncomprehending, limiting,

So many choose to wear it,
At some age, raise the pondering form
Above them and set it on,
Then disconnect the growing form within.

It is the age that offer its style,
Whose future generation marvel
At the quaint styles dropped as the age
Pass itself out, its trinkets obsolete.

Unfitting now to forms who wonder
How the disguise fit, how the bindings chafed,
Along the outer selves who trussed
And stepped unconsciously.

It was their protocol to form,
While within, the possibility
Of nakedness lie dormant, sleeping in some drugged state,
Twisting upon nightmare dreams
Of madding hallucination trance.

(2007)

The Bones of Timeless Stars

We are the stars, though view the stars,
An oval mirror spread into reflection
Upon itself, the cold eternals
Just out of comprehension, out of reach.

We are the bones of timeless stars,
Whose sounds like steely voices pierce us
When at solitude. Frozen fire leaping
Past our senses, through us radiate

Like sound waves. To tune them
Is the magic possible at sense,
Though language falter, mind eclipse,
Thought ramble aimlessly, and

Body machine, its momentary heat
Shiver at the darkness which expose
The vision of their majesty, a glimpse
Into the span of consciousness.

(2007)

Our Experience as Selves

Behind the gods are selves
Creating footing that we may look out
Upon stars, as if on firmament,
As if at home where we belong.

The selves restrict us, that to paths
We form, wearing, rutting grooves along
As our momentary consciousness ignite
As some dim phosphorescent vapor light

To view the spacious universe
In droplets. We view ourselves
Looking into selves which are distinct
In some form, then extending to touch,

To join what awareness separate.
To yearn, to grasp, to hoard at beauty
That we discover past our fingertips,
To contain passion, then compassion,
Then a seeming shepherd quality.

This is our experience as selves.
This is our hearth which sustain us,
This is our delight beyond emotion
That bridge our innocence and wisdom as one.

(2007)

Fires Which are Cold

I am the light of fires which are now cold.
Their place on hills long ago blazed,
Warm then, piercing at night
To their stewards, who plied them at the air.

They are dark and silent now,
The peaks forgotten to this age,
Who do not tend them,
Do not look out to distant luminosity,

Since they are blinded of glare
From their own devices,
That heat a feverish sweat upon them
As they seek to look
At what is hidden from their dim experience.

I am another kind of light of old,
That swept as magic, into primal eyes,
Reflecting a sincerity of oneness with a few
Who climbed to make the pyre.

Who refracted from darkness, yellow beams,
To gods who were inside themselves,
Who, aching to become exposed,
Burst full into enlightenment.

(2007)

Contemplation

We are not far from grace who stand alone
In silent rapture at the day,
In still rooms where the moment
Is all there is of life.

And we are forgotten, no place in worlds
To cling where activity rules,
No home among the masses
Whose lives are controlled by louding noise.

There is no record here that we have been,
Whose growth, like trees, is not noticed
Till their great boughs shade over
Generations passing by,

With such effort, who never looked up,
So difficult were their lives.
But we effortlessly expand around them
In a different sort of life.

Here, where perception of quiet fills us
Like snow covering us,
Like water covering us,
Brings peace, and movement, like death, is done.

(2002)

The Gods' Hill

I rally to the ledgers seeking cold sobriety.
Their vellum pages smooth like cotton sheets
To weary flesh, sought as refuge to repose.
Simple as air, strong as gale or sudden still.

Here it is the gods' hill I climb,
Here the passage to infinity,
No mere mortal seek. No untempered youth
Can climb it, no unscarred pretender to a life.

It is the vision to awakening,
Static frustration damped out,
Old ties released like dried mud
Falling away as dark at swamps, I rise.

It is the gliding of the pen,
Sweet celestial sound ancients felt,
Which cleared their thickened forms,
Stole fire where the black had been their sight.

And what put? What clogged channel
Could express the wakened self to communicate,
To drive golden spear points
Through sweated chests?

To release blood's flow, to spill out
Into unexpressed, unknown spaces
That are not imagined, unfelt,
Not sensed.

What said releases them? What pain
Can inflict, or pleasure ignite, logic spark,
Calm, or peace, enchantment, dream produce,
When silence is the core of them?

(2006)

The Urge to Emulate

The urge to emulate enlightenment
Is what holds, finally remains,
Consistent, even past touch and sparkl'd things,
Past air, just further than light.

The quiet still, the reach convention shun,
The letting go of firmament for invisibility,
Where dimensions spin, *auf klarung* start,
And sound a silence which expose a tone

Of life, simple to experience when belief alter
From noise, to quiet, from speak, to act,
From expectation, to momentary experience,
And nature, rise, bold and brisk,

Hard cutting, strip'd blade to glint
Its steady course, its cycle begin again
To return itself, its self things
To grow finally into our soulful realms.

(2006)

To be Whole

It is not magic to be whole,
Swamp things achieve it,
Molecules encircle it, balanc'd galaxies project
What it is to do what they are.

Though we are made of them, exhibit
Other qualities, hungry, when full,
Lonely, when crowded,
Expressive, when alone,

The ability to touch, a slap,
The lingering glaze, a glare,
Comfort, a confinement, perfection, passing,
Beauty corrupting, noise erupting,

Infrastructure crumbling. We grasp
And are healed. We possess
And are cleansed. We take
And are absolved,

We desire and are freed,
We accumulate and are blessed,
We linger on the circular path of life,
To adjust our load, and steady on.

(2006)

Now Inner Prowling Come

The silence speak, night things,
Dark things in memory,
When predators were available to pounce,
Now, inner prowling come.

Inner hunger run beasts, some blood
Awaken them, some scent alert them,
Some terror embolden them to stalk
Within, the primal synapse field.

The gray flesh tempt them to appear,
To form in it, foul in it,
Beneath the eyes delve in it,
Twist worm-like through it,

And not asleep, or awake, prevent it,
Dreams not dispel or drug dull,
Not activity defer, not sensation,
The process activate

And play itself out.
It is the curse of silence to be vulnerable,
But noise obliterate the self, shatter sobriety
Into an agony of base vibration, where the thoughtless dwell.

(2006)

What has Returned

What has returned, sweet light,
Though not light, not that brightened thing
Which separates, but this is light in dark
As if eyes were beast-like clear,

And could dispel the silence of a night.
I am that liquid form come through.
I can perceive the maleness now in me,
Warming everything I felt was cold,

Becoming comfortable in flesh.
What had been desire, now possessed,
What agony in slights, now repelled,
And put away like childish things.

The patience of life preserve its heart,
Final, thoughtless compassion of humanity,
Its unconscious beauty, that to behold
In this clarity, dissolves its illusion of conformity,

And I can now grope what is beyond my hand,
That I did not fashion into real,
That I did not embody as myself,
That just beyond, continues its strange gleam.

The Faded Bride, About to Rise

Though past hope, some settled place
Where it must be home, as homes
I knew are dissipated into synapse corridors,
I lie, the faded bride, about to rise.

And go now, go to the rooms of gown
Where I am drawn like compasses
To magnetic finery that slide upon me as other skin,
In some terrible longing to be whole,

In unity of parts, simplicity of satisfaction
Like magic gems, its nest sparkled
Like artic snowdust, it nests.

I rest in the possession of higher things,
Transcending things, what to experience in them,
Their doorway inexpressible, not shared,
Not entrance or departure to other realms,

Not warm, their glittering termperatures unlike
Some warm touch at other places of me
Which are in aching need, this ability to dress
Does not look outward, but far in

To clothe the Adam from his nakedness,
Who stands inside me shivering,
Undetected in grim society, my private debutant
About to step, in me.

(2005)

Isolation of Inner Self

The isolation of inner self is silent to us,
And we cannot compare it to a thing,
Or remove it for speculation,
Or join it to another being.

It is the one cool sun
That illuminates even light,
Enhances brightness, yet we do not shield ourselves
Because it does not burn the eyes.

It is the sign of clarity few can grasp,
The lonely trail which in itself is life,
Its movement quiet and slow because it is not warm,
It does not follow moths to glow.

It does not dip in nature's heat,
Supple male forms cannot detract it,
Only shadow where it is relieved from view,
To see, or be seen, without the distraction of sight.

(2001)

The Still is at an Equinox

Wait soft, the still is at an equinox,
And we are silent at the forest,
Hoping now the woodlike passion come,
Like animal initiate, and we at full,
Expose ourselves upon the plane.
Learner of the special ways,
Where we grasp at paw to know.

(1976)

Just a Thing

To be just a thing
As tiny as a word,
And send it out like demons to destruction,
Like arrows heading in,

Like darts with all the venom dipped,
As plentiful as air,
And all the ease is in the making,
With breath for implement.

And where our hopeless target stands,
We strike each moment down,
And load ourselves with silent pleasure,
Sent incidentally.

(1976)

The Sound

I thought I had gone all to sleep,
The stars were still where they belong,
And I so tired since the morning
Took me into day.

But then, I heard the strangest sound,
Not like the tick inside,
Unusual, some like a flower
Blooming in the dark.

I checked the locks, and they were sound,
I fumbled with a lamp,
I thought I heard the shadows moving
Round that something, thing.

I pulled the covers round my heart,
I touched my eyes to see,
And waited at the silence growing,
And my breath was still.

Some earthless figure was within,
I sensed it breathe about the air,
And brush my cheek without me feeling,
Then gone as easily.

(1976)

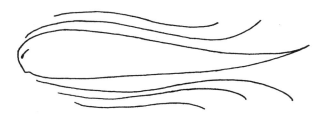

We Just Forget

We just forget the loneliest,
The day is not so long,
And sweep our dusty space in thinking,
Almost into hope.

And then the gods are at our door,
And beams are everywhere,
And we are burnished with the lightning,
And go blind within.

The searing touch of quality,
A terror just as grand as loss,
To meet one morning, at an apron,
In such a little room.

(1976)

Upon the Ocean

As if some bird upon the ocean stopped to drink,
And questioned there the drinks to have,
And whether thirsting on an ocean
Nulled the thought to drink.

And whether to be drowned in thirst,
Flying beneath the waves,
Its beak closed firmly
At such a common generosity.

Remembering at forest where it failed,
Where it would all have given feathers for a drop,
And thankless came the sun to it, to burn,
With light, in magnitude.

And somehow it survived without,
Its faith now on itself to choose alone
The quality of circumstances for its need,
That rise superior.

(1976)

Some Fates

Some fates enchant us with themselves,
They spin etheric as the moon,
And spend a constant vision on our solitude,
And beam occasional.

A light to make us prettier,
A chance amid the glen,
To sit in special moments with a happiness,
We hold into ourselves.

Sometimes the fortunes are at peace.
We brush a quiet by,
And check with special apron at the mid lit day,
And put a smilefull comfort on.

And rest, the storms are far away,
And we may venture, having been so saved,
Where once we hid the shutters round the terror sound,
And thought our body hardly more than to withstand.

(1976)

A Hardening

As if I could not bear the day,
It came more gentle in,
And spread me with its yellow beams, and lighted air,
As if an offering of balm, by sympathy.

And yet the pain had never gone.
Its hold so monumental in a little self,
My court of blood and endings round it hardly held
So tensing, that I dared not move, to burst.

And bulged within my everything,
An agony so smooth,
It melted to the corners of my hidden mind,
And touched me like a giant's press.

And then I felt a hardening,
As if to stone became,
And weathered to forever like the mountains,
And just as silent, disappeared.

(1976)

Now Dreaming

Now dreaming, but would I wake,
The world would on its hinges roll
Into me as a flower blooming million selves,
And I a stroke of majesty.

And each hand, lips would kiss into,
From men, all deities,
As beautiful as summer rolled in instants,
And every one for me.

And stand as greatest as a thought
Of peace in agony,
Until eternity extinguished,
And fragments disappeared.

(1976)

To the World

I bring a vision to the earth
That daffodils would know,
And mosses in the forest listen,
And blossoms in a tree.

And ones that have no other thing to do,
Would take the magic in,
And regulate it to perfection,
And hold it like a bulb.

For generations in the green
To have another bloom,
And scientist to check it, listed,
In just another book.

(1976)

I Drift to Inches

Simple as the, tiny, things,
I drift to inches vast,
And comment on the changes there,
That seem an ultimate.

I toil great leaves of, brittle grass,
And see a world expand,
Mighty as the petal bending,
And gentle as the air.

I feel how tall visions of the Age,
That Grand, and busy lot,
Seem unnecessary, cautious,
And were as pain to tell.

As less there is to do, in Time,
There is the more to have,
So settle on the moment, projected,
And dream that there are Stars.

Style Was Out

I thought to love, but style was out,
And so I fumbled through the day,
And wound my hair in simple thought,
And smoothed a petticoat.

And stationed by the door, as if in hope,
And rigid as the light, to wait,
Stood silent till the darkness entered,
And left me wondering.

As if a move might bring him then,
Or light the window shade,
Or wait until the moon had risen
And lit my simple stare.

(1978)

I Sing the Song

I sing the song of Sodomy,
Which you would sing to me,
Were you my man love under me,
Soft notes which you would sing,

Entering in consummation,
Spreading you until into you, losing
Faint control, I lose myself,

As I feel the entering.
You are my male fuck whole man
Being, you are my heat
Into my cock, raging what you are.

I madly press until I cannot hold you more,
You are my madness come,
My scream, to arch my back in you
I come, I come, my man male, come.

This is some rugged act of love,
Is that which hearts shall hold,
Which ache is meaning to be felt,
To grasp into your ass,

My fingers pressing on your self,
My passion to be mated into you,
You cannot stop this raging male musk,
Pounding into what is us, and us.

Wisdom Deep

We had joined as something mystical,
Without limitations, without blinders on,
And feeling at our fingertips,
That we were wisdom deep.

We embraced, then, two gods
On altar bed, gods performing an old ritual,
Driven into them.

And each gash was a love hole,
Their thrusts were spikes in pounding heat,
Were sharpened blades, seared rough,
And we moaned a roaring sound.

So that was love.
I can't find that once so overwhelming
State of place,
How to mount that aged divide,
To reach into that source of it.

I can't ascend to that paradise,
Where I was once immortalized,
And all the worshippers were mine, and mine,
And fire altar, flesh flames,
Once burned heavenward to me.

(2000)

Fire

Lean back, and take my arms
Around you, beloved,
And there, campfire light
Upon us, let me hold you.

Let whatever moments pass there
Be not yours or mine, but one.
Beyond the galaxies, or step,
Before the microcosm,

Be one from you and me.
Body heat and breath be our food and drink,
Silence be our whispering,
Heartbeat pulse our blood.

We are young again, and free,
And do not need, or clutch, or bind,
And do not seek
Beyond the moments passing there.

What is our life, is what is love,
As firelight is heat.
We lean into the warming place,
Not from the cold.

We are not driven to the heat,
For it must be within to feel,
Be there already, and letting go,
Consumes us like the wood.

(2000)

Ourselves

Something in the hills went out,
And though the trees were green,
And mosses round in fashion at the solitude,
And birds inside the air,

And memory intact, I felt the loss.
As if a smallest creature died,
Its only need unsatisfied, unnoticed,
By the sun, or greater majesties.

And everything at pace went on,
As casual, to me, as inches on a vastness,
Where the slightest move is incidental,
The momentary life dissolves.

(1976)

The Waiting

The waiting is as wonderful
As hope upon a light,
When we are sinking in the darkness,
Knowing we are safe.

As anxious as a letter held,
Imagining the joy it must have sealed,
And all the consequence is ours,
And all our deeds are done.

And we are ready for the bliss,
The visitors may come,
And wonder at the pride we offer,
Because our trial is through.

(1976)

Another Battle Done

Mellow, sadness, is like a sea,
With tiara and, bracelet, on,
Then, hush.

Her perfume whips all, senses,
Like a gorgon she tears at my clothes
Till I fall, submerged, in her fancy.

With another battle, done,
I'll leave the cold,
And swim towards home.

(1968)

My Silence

My silence was as big to me
As everything I wished,
And on it felt how deep my emptiness had dropped,
Like stones we put in wells.

And then I held my ears from it,
The distance terrified,
For such a little hand to test it,
And so impossible to fill.

(1976)

Upon the Hillside

Sky comes upon the hillside dressed in blue,
To where I linger, dipped in day,
And memoried in dream and thought
Of once, where I had better been.

And passes as I gaze beyond each valley at below,
And down the mountain lights are faded,
Where the cold permeates in its hush,
A push, and I am gone into my heated room.

(1976)

I Saw Him

I saw him in the mountains,
And then, into the sea,
And looked around the world for clues,
Wherever he might be.
I checked into an old hotel
With news that he'd be there,
But found the record of his death,
By an overdose, of me.

(1969)

Amid These Rooms

Amid these rooms I lie,
So close to hidden fortunes
Whose glitter lures me
Like a mystic scent.

Their beauty like majesty,
The royal heads that must have worn
These crowns, such secrets
That I would forget myself to know,

And place the golden circlets round,
And fit the heavy rings in place.
I would all forfeit, all that be,
In mind and memory,

To lay myself in this other world
Where everything comes true,
And we are capable of holding,
And keeping, long enough.

(1977)

Memories of Hope

As usual as memory of hope,
I make a special room,
And lay my better sorrows down there,
Trailing out of date.

And paint a special smile upon,
And go out in the day,
And terror in my gusts of loneliness,
And weary in the light.

And tremble in my heart, a sigh,
So long it would affect eternity.
And sink me if the ground would open,
And null all consciousness.

(1977)

Veiled Upon the Earth

Veiled upon the earth, I search,
My pilgrims are come back to life,
And to them, in my mind, send unknown things
That they may follow to me, and my temples light!

I am the goddess of eternity,
And age to age return upon my holy land
In prayer brought wisdom, for my people to return
As they have always been.

I wait to be alive to them!
Their greatness shall arise again
In silent moon tide perfectness,
And they shall leave the earth for sky.

All the waters shall arise,
And all the land be mine,
I rule it as I judge the elements therein,
And push them into use.

(1977)

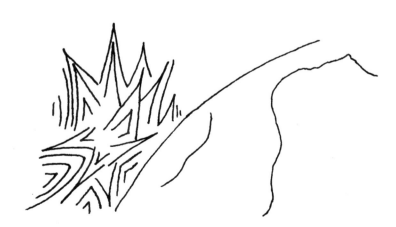

Our Dreamlike Spin

We are pushed deeply out of selves
When the moments of our dreamlife spin, unmanned,
Touched darkly on horizons that we fail to know,
Where there were temples, gone to dust.

Follow if you dare, the light
Upon the other side of beam,
Where it demands a pagan sacrifice,
And you are altar bound!

Alone, rebuild the palaces to worship secretly.
You are the priestess now, as ever been,
Holy in the sight of this silver light,
And sacred to the moon.

Her black face is a hidden gem,
A terror powerful as will,
To spread the veil into the house of no return,
Where you must senseless go.

(1977)

The Wondering

Unheard of in the wondering,
The simple lie as unexposed as thought,
As magic as a wish,
As volatile as glee.

Or mystic as touch from deities,
They herald in the gladness,
On miles of oaken rooms
Where we play our little moments,

Where the edge of breath lie,
We bear so near our consciousness,
As fine as eider breath,
And then we wake.

(1977)

Sing Song Bell

Sing song bell, the child is in the well,
And none will come to save her,
And she will go to hell,
And sister will inherit all,

And friends will come to play.
Oh let us watch the child go down,
And we will eat on spice and tea,
And go down to the shore,

And meet a laughing crowd,
Of joyous revelers,
Who dance to tunes of melody,
And frolic as none before.

Until we are so satisfied,
Will join the raucous crew,
Then come back sober as a pike
And live as others do.

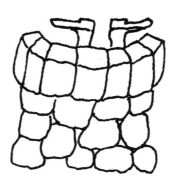

The Dark

So distant in the hills I lie,
Awakened by the cold, and ravaged,
Helpless for myself to move,
And thoughtless where I am.

And hurt, somehow alive, though still,
I listen at the forest for a sound
Of safe, but nothing
But internal throbbing, out of time.

Crazed somehow, a cracked wing in the brain,
To beat some horror tune
At bulged nerves, slowly changing out of shape,
To cause a dumb wall pushed out at the dark.

(1977)

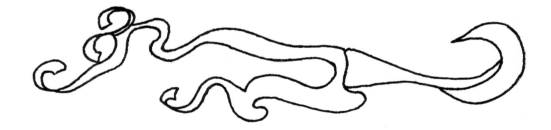

The Deep

The horror house is silent in the night,
When there is sleep, like frozen dreams,
So old in their still silent faces,
Gleaming in the old.

No magic now, the clocks are full,
Too sluggish to be stepping past
A tick, into unthought of land,
Too dangerous for hope.

Now only sleep, the remnant of that
Once ago where dreams came lightly
Into form, and there was light enough
To join the fire and the flame.

Each hand for hand, this memory
Of distant gems like ones a lady wore,
Like guideposts, as we bump upon them,
Between the monsters and the deep.

(1977)

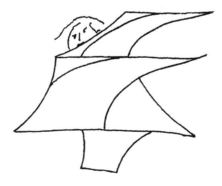

Before the Sun

Some others stop before the sun,
Their lessons are of gold,
They have a worldly magnitude,
And question everyone.

Mine is just beside the hill,
Where beams may end and stay,
Where petals are a bliss, or ruin,
And grass is counted out.

A soft of velvets, a hush of crown,
A richness none compare who own it,
And those who grasp the shining glare
Are moving into light.

The bright illumine them,
And they reflect, while we remain,
To smooth the few examples of our stay,
In shadow, and still, and done.

(1978)

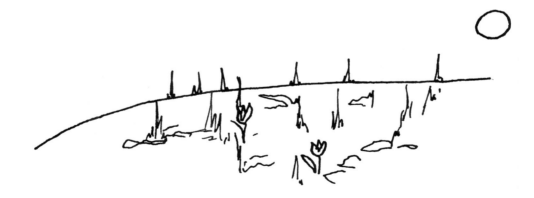

There is a Haunting

There is a haunting in the stillness,
Come like tugging at the hem,
When I am waiting at the door for hope,
Silent within the room.

Like shadows in the dark that sweep
Upon a skin as touch,
And somewhere deep a shudder tremble,
As if it knew the thing.

And remember when the room was full,
When we could spread our natures at the field,
And scream a vision to the heavens,
That shriek infinity!

Here lies the creature that we knew,
Who has not spoken for centuries in us,
And lay as a leaden child in a womb,
And spread slow poison to the brain.

Unheard of since we were in this silent room,
Its being, useless, but a prick
To give us memory of station, of the time
When there was more.

(1978)

The Golden Ages Lie Asleep

The golden ages lie asleep this equinox,
Gods are out of style, the temples few
In rocky places where I step,
On some outcropping, in some sea.

What heavy thickness is this crown,
Such weight upon my head,
Valuable as magic, solitary symbol,
Some survival form on me,

Which girds me past the terror house,
That bind me in the light,
As rarefied as sparkle in a darkness,
As precious as delight.

As holy as a thought of safe,
When we are journey bound,
To free myself upon this landscape
Of eternal sleep.

(1978)

Each Day

Each day extends its frugal light
To show what it has brought,
And we, intent discoverers
May catalog the plan.

To check and mark each article,
To section by its hue,
And situate and calculate,
And mark the beings down.

(1978)

Silent

We are silent in the world
Who shutter out the light,
And hide behind a velvet curtain,
And sink into the folds.

And dream, a fortune at our touch,
Each move a different world,
Contented to be at our fingers,
And we content to stay.

(1978)

The Destroyed Teddy Bear

Boy, loved him with a touch,
And had him tiny things,
Where they'd go to check them out,
On woodpiles rotting, cherishing.

Mother secret, was the villain,
That her child, she misunderstood,
Starting in an inquisition
Of the childhood, perishing.

His wishes never spread too far,
Destroyed as they were made,
And children slipping by the damage
Never quite repair themselves.

(1970)

Survivors

Survivors past the ancient wreck
Find saved a simple thing,
With space for other memories
And room to rest a moment in.

And time to brush the floor and sigh,
And lean out on a ledge,
And find the quiet incidental,
And stop with just a breath.

And feel as if they are whole again,
Limbs seem same, and pain away
Would leave them almost satisfaction
That this safe is true.

But somewhere past the eyes in them,
A bent hinge slap upon a dark,
And they remember falling, failing,
And then the grasp is dim.

And then they think of other storms,
Ruined, sunk to as they fled,
And with it, past all hope of saving,
Went particle of life.

(1978)

We Fear the Beast Within

How we fear the beast within,
Its tentacles of strength surround,
Yet we are barren in its grasp,
Our lips are hard and dry.

Our fingers reach beyond its hold,
A hope to paradise,
That could free us from its lurking,
Where there would be release.

Where dark would not affect the land,
Where moon, a plastic thing,
Would shine just for our whim, or set,
And go out as we please.

But I am other places gone, to different luxury,
To soothe the raging of these beings,
To make a monster camp
And fill it with myself.

To lock the garden from the world,
And smooth the burden out,
And when the terrors come in blackness,
Kiss them with a knowing touch.

(1978)

In This Room of Day

So quiet in this room of day,
It seems the creatures gone,
And sun is moving like a particle,
And I am same.

And feel forgotten things,
Today that cheer the walls,
And are a company,
And warm upon myself.

Remembering, the once ago, in life,
The remnants of a greatness I put on,
And sit in velvets that the ancients wore,
And feel a tug within.

And know the path to it is just the past,
And shallow are the moments by,
That there, dwell on it, barely formed,
To bring to consciousness.

But still, familiar comes,
And hums some simple song
That taps upon my brain like fingers,
And wants to take me in.

(1978)

We Stood Helpless Once

The agony still waits inside
Of when we could not scream,
Of when the terrors came too quickly,
And we stood helpless once.

Waiting for a madness to release,
Anticipating fall, though we had thought
The wounds were scar now,
The danger past ourselves.

The wreck just memory, or souvenir
We had clutched, now with diamond hands,
Amuse the thought of our destruction,
Giggle to the fate.

But hidden stronger than our lives,
A crush prepared to land,
We thought had limited to passing,
But pass on us one time again.

(1978)

Different Now

At mad, the world seem sane,
The horrors that unstrung us,
Still beat into our brains,
The heaviness that weight us, still there.

But we are different now, the room says so,
Its silence like an eye on us,
And we are helpless to be hidden
From the staring that we know.

We are different now, says land,
Its tree a stranger, moss away,
And we may step on barren,
Like our senses that have bent somehow.

We may not rest, the damage done,
Removes a chance of thought
That hope is like a godly planchet,
And we are worthy to receive.

(1978)

Stilled Now

Stilled now, the time stops,
And like eternity, prolong,
A loss like keys of monumental,
Like temples crumbling.

And so alone, the moments reach
Like shroud upon ourselves,
And we have hardly room,
The little cottage shrinking past the ache.

And as we stand, just noticing,
Our burden crush like earth's
Forgotten axis in our spine,
And we condemned to stand,

And take the weights all in like day
Surround us so, and thoughtless
To our capability or hope,
Demand till we have felt.

(1978)

The Thought of Still

Not greatness has this life become,
The cask is plain like smooth,
And on it lie, no passion
Past the thought of still.

No movement come, no sound,
Except the day remind me
Of something that I seem to know,
Could seem to spark the moments,

Stilled now, like dark in warm,
But I am too far from animal
To sense the missing thing,
Too distant from a beast-like roar.

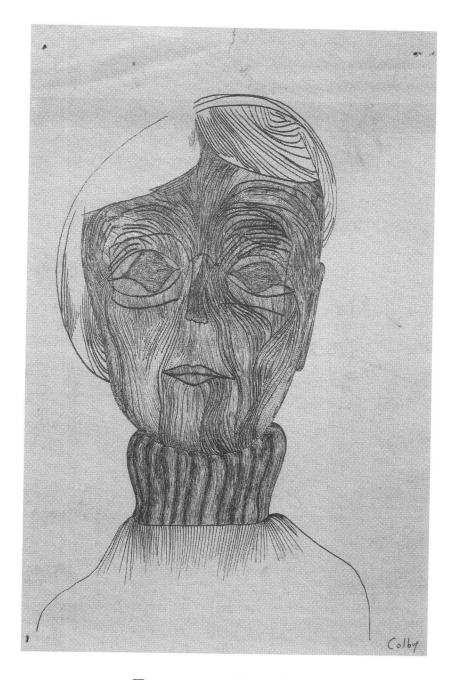

Poet as a Youth

A Warming In

We are at distant to an older life,
The bee and clover done,
The gardens walled like fortresses,
The mansions locked away.

The forest, particle of memory,
Of when the moss and pine
Gave breath of vapor like a sudden hush,
Like sunlight breaking through.

As when the cottage, dipped in snow,
Extend its powdered hand,
And we once may have reached the sight
In simple expectation,
And taste a warming in.

(1978)

Agonize in Gem

Sometimes the thought, like an ache,
Come deep as memories of loss,
And shake the ages placed in between,
Where we have hidden from the terror house.

It lingers like a vapor when we sense,
And trickle to our brain,
Like we had never passed the horror station
All those centuries at pace.

To run into oblivion, the form still linger,
And we are its subject where we lie,
And suffer in our golden laces,
And agonize in gem.

(1978)

The Wonder Lands

Oh, to join the wonder lands,
Where there is sometimes fame,
Where joy condense in particles,
And spread a shower down.

And goodness start,
It seem participants are of gold,
And sun direct them to its shining,
And fortify their gleam.

And they turn towards us like an age,
We may see everything,
And feel a pulse or likeness by their gift,
Each word a life to us.

Each thought or phrase, the world renew,
In gladness for the thing,
And while we linger into stillness,
The greatness goes louding on.

And in my room of eider soft,
I turn these wordlings round,
And hold them like a pearl, that merchants
Know the value of.

(1978)

Omen

What fear is this, so silent creep upon me,
As if it brought some gentle news,
Or were to share its goodly secret,
Only one may hear,
Standing as an omen, at my side?

Should I guess it,
Or speak the creature in ghostly language to,
And find its harbinged tale gust out,
Or let it creep, and from the sight,
Relieve myself to know,
Only what portend a skying change,
When birds are low.

(1973)

Like Pages

This life, like pages, wait for air,
Perhaps each century, until the follower
Begin to touch, so many hopes,
From souvenir, and fail.

This is where I died that thought,
This word, my last embrace,
This, begin to drop a little,
The moments were so long.

This mark, a lifetime of my wait,
This space a desperate pause,
Until my fingers crack like sounds
Eternities contain.

And so I spend the room till then,
Where I may have enough
To link one last goodbye,
To where I am, and gone.

(1978)

Past the Thought of Room

I have sunken past the thought of room,
My vehicle for life, where majesty,
Like chairs, stand out for moment then,
Or happenstance to sit.

And I each breath fall pageward down,
To think in meter or in rhyme, for hope
Of thought, or some salvation,
Like lamps when we are dark.

And futureward glance, each drop,
For hope of when the light is clear,
We may still shine, we may still glisten
In the need of some.

(1978)

Into the Still

Into the still I sit and listen at the day,
Unthought of reverie from nature, come
Majestic in its hold to singularity,
A moment magnified in touch.

And on it hold, inebriate of fellowship,
I join the simple link in silent bliss,
And deep into the sinews, marking
Where I come, a glance of hope.

Promise of my station, out of date,
Still mine, crowns of diadem advance,
And wrap me, mingled in my trueness
To the glory thing, a grand embark.

And I am ready here in web,
My dews adorn where gem more fine
Than solid, find worthy, sitting round
The spherey orb, a glorious deserve.

(1978)

The Skies had Changed

It was as if the skies had changed,
And feeling at an edge
Came like an omen to my silence,
And brought the moments in.

And slowly there I checked them round,
And counted all the ones,
And set them to myself in waiting
For what this storm might bring.

(1978)

Left Out

I thought I were a, widower,
Foot said, so,
Stepping into lonely streets,
Shiny leathered, virgin, toe.

And then I thought, survivor
Is what I must, be,
From some old wreck,
Or accident, now safe.

Perhaps when, stars, changed places,
And danced on crowded floor,
I was left, out,
Adopted here.

(1969)

Mysteries of Grace

Easy from the sane
To go, and hoop a skirt along,
Beyond a sensibility and reason,
Beyond a happy rhyme.

Now capable of strangest things,
Now necessary to observe,
And catalog in easy labels,
To place so safe away.

And scrub the spot where I had been
In some sobriety,
And paint a little smile,
And lift it into cages by a wall,
And lock the thing away.

Now to my returning, gone the key,
That need to keep me here,
And to the crazy house I wander,
For mysteries of grace.

(1978)

To Check Infinity

I think the most of night, is hid,
For people, not to see.
They'd count and number draws of it,
For souls who, couldn't come.

They'd sit with rule, in chambers,
To check, infinity,
A darkness that has passed them,
And given some to, me.

(1969)

The Notes Clear Ring

To be as Great as I had been,
Would take another World,
And if I could pretend, forgetting,
Would reach the Royal site.

To be explaining, bounds of Self,
That arch the highest, low,
Then contemplate, expressing wholeness,
Qualities of all.

I would be as I were, intact,
Except destruction sings,
The melody that all can fathom,
Unless for them, the notes clear ring.

(1971)

Our Sense

How dangerous our sense lie,
To scoop an agony,
Or raise some simple hope in greatness,
Or regulate a heart.

Or stand like jewels thrown into mobs,
With air turned into hands to grasp,
And load us with a weight of losses,
And sink into a mire.

And dull, and blind, and mix an ear,
So it can only hold, like funnels,
And fill us with a groan of horror,
While we turn into pain.

(1978)

Inside a Silent Room

I sit inside a silent room,
Protected like a jewel,
Tucked softly in some hideaway
Where neither loud, nor common, come.

And on each side, a wall of safe,
Doors to lock, and curtains draw,
And stay as still as moment,
And wait, for thing to do.

And hope, if summer come, or light,
And dream at stars, and moon,
And twist in stiffened hands
A reason to be through.

(1978)

The Beast

The beast is unlike anything
The senses have thought of,
No danger for the muscle come,
No fear for weaponry.

No danger for the house, or goods,
It come like nightly snow,
And soft us while unnoticing,
And cover heavily.

No scream can pry it, movement out,
No anguish alter then,
No shovel chase the whitening,
Or clear, where yesterday

We chance to go with ease, or cause.
This dark snow now induce itself
Almost ethereal upon our being,
And to return is done.

And what we were, becomes,
So like a century ago,
Stiff in ancient form unknown,
Strange in foreign gowns of lace.

The thing, now like a majesty
Control our sense,
And like a childish souvenir,
What we knew, remove to drawers for memory.

(1978)

Careless Landscape

And so I shut the door on want,
Its careless landscape dangerous
With animal not in a book,
Or poison plant invisible to touch.

And paths there leading where you want to go
If you are strong enough,
And victims used for stones in building
A palace for your mighty crown.

I bolt the door, and never in
This doom world, in its fashion go,
Till I am mindless to this thought of travel,
And sense thrown out in chains.

(1978)

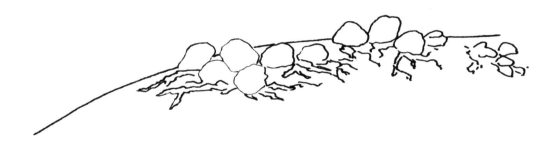

The Noticing

A tug somewhere behind my breast,
As if reminder of the day
I put these heavy velvets on,
And weighted in my room of day.

And sunk behind the oak, and rug,
And felt circumference come
And stiff me in,
And tighten till I squeezed.

Pulled gentle like a fashion, then,
I was unable to unhook
The pinions on me,
And the place, less noticed now,
The spot spun like a gauze of veil.

My lips once pressed into thought
Of what the feeling had been before,
To my breath one moment come,
And then the noticing is done.

(1978)

It is like Agony

It is like agony we cannot feel,
And yet the damage come,
Somewhere like rooms of houses
That have gone to weather, since a century.

We did not notice that the lands were dry,
And that we could not think somehow of family.
It is like generations that we had come from,
And ancients tell us memories.

We did not know we had been lost,
Or loss a thing so grand,
There could not be a space for else,
Until the pang, like death,

Now open senses that we had been closed,
And all the blur dissolve like tiredness,
And we are fresh, and wiser,
Like an age had passed that day.

(1978)

At the Deepest of Myself

This beating at the deepest of myself
Is hardly sound to day,
Its drum-like constancy for seeming centuries,
Attracts me like a foreign gauge.

As if the motors were forgot,
And I ran onward like a wheel,
Now ignorant of its revolve
And sources from the turn.

As if I did not know myself,
A slipping into consciousness,
That is as sleeplike as my memories,
And is depending on a sense.

And still there is the sound I tell
Into myself for hope,
That might connect me to the centers,
To answer such a call.

(1978)

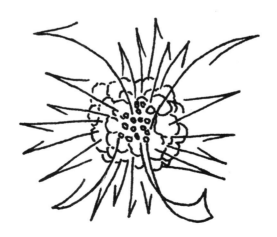

This Crown

What burden now to wear this crown,
Of broken stones and lead,
That I had once assumed was Glory,
With just the putting on.

And searched forever, so it seemed,
To clutch the circlet round,
And pin it on my head for majesty,
Then turn to reach the world.

But they were all in gold, and Spice,
In autumn, and afternoons,
And took eternity for moments,
To drink from silver bowls.

I did not know the language, there,
And struggle still with, ands, and, so,
And saw them all prepared, ascending,
On beyond, and on.

And I remain, so just alone,
No earth, man speak to me,
As if I had no right to prosper,
Not being native, in his society.

(1973)

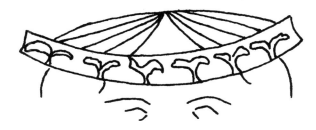

Things to Do

I dreamed that, there were things to Do,
And I had every one,
Calling in and out of Rooms,
For materials, to bind.

Then there were holocausts, and Me at hand,
To gird at every move,
Met the ruins, hand to hand,
And turned the beings round.

And for my good, came greater things,
And for the Grace of that,
Saw the time move universal,
And put each century, in Row.

And found old Scriptures, crumbling,
That spoke eternity,
And in a pause, there read the moment
That spoke of Gods, like me.

(1973)

I Did Fly

I was a bird, and I did fly,
Upon a petaled wing,
Tracts and drafts were kindest then,
And everywhere to go.

I had a silken tree to land,
Of crystal, and of wood.
I had a golden worm to eat,
Dipped in Alabaster bowls.

Rose was life, and I was thin,
A crescent for my brow,
And oh, I never touched the landscape,
But all the trees, did bow.

I Wore a Jewel

I wore a Jewel, but just afraid,
Exchanged it, with a glass,
Incidental of the Value,
It fit me just the same.

Afraid that it, would wear and tarnish,
Exchanged it for a day,
And gave Eternity an instant
To gasp, then carry on.

(1972)

A Self

I am faithful to a self I know
That has no certain name,
It comes as innocent as season,
To tree that readies, silently.

All deep within, a careful inch,
The layers all like gauze of steel,
We could not penetrate for trying,
The know come from a memory,

When we were just the core inside.
Our consciousness come from ready need,
And yet, just unnoticed,
Sifting on, covering in dust,

Till lines are gone the ancients knew,
And we must all depend on hopeful feel
Of what the greatness be inside,
So sacred, to be so removed.

(1978)

Within the Dark

Within the dark, some night, at last,
We stand amid the rooms,
Our pulsing spreading to all senses,
Step within the space,

And heavy, remove our ancient coats
In silent presence of our solitude,
Wait, the day shall never fill this place
Till we are gone.

Our morning fog like wet, are one,
Laid over like a wave come in,
And we are still, forever rocklike
Thickness.

But feeling come upon us then,
And opening of shrill delight,
To melt the weightiness, as sudden
As light exterminate a gloom.

When We Were Grand

In a memory of past,
We touch the ancient hem,
And feel the bodice where it used to tug
When we were grand.

Forgotten as the youth to dust that he became
Some century, we linger at the bustle,
In a pause, almost remembering the feel,
And then the mind examine

Its bloated self, to its ruin from that time.
How slim the waist that filled that spot,
What tiny knee bent round this seam,
And hand beyond this cuff.

Too big somehow we stretch the fit,
And force our spreading thighs along the satin
And choke into the blouse we wore that century,
And crush into the tiny shoes that tie,

And try to simulate the once ago,
For fear that when we come to glory in our gown,
The god may not remember what we were,
Or we may not remember, having swollen out of size

(1978)

A Stopless Wind

It was as if a century
Had gone, while I was away,
And clocks repeating to my sense
Ticked out the mystery.

Each change was unknown, as if the loss
Was in smaller things than molecule,
Unnoticed, though my body still retained
The same importance of a need, or grace.

But the place I knew, was gone.
I move unsteadily, my motion halt,
And I in strangeness, like a foreigner,
Try to grasp on some familiar thing.

And unto my furtherest travels, in its reaches
Am alone, as thought is all unhooked,
To face this new world, crazed
In a madness, like a stopless wind.

(1978)

Upon the Oaken Rooms, was Grand

Into caverns, that some primal holllow grew
Out of the earth, I lie,
None shall fathom where the depth begin,
In tonnage of granite, like tomb.

I lie here where there are no sounds, but thought,
Akin to darkness in this smallest room,
Prevent me from becoming stone,
And like an ancient trinket,
Linger past the century.

And like the stillness, I feel almost at peace.
Then there is just the faintest pause
Behind the brain,
Reminding me of some once ago,
When I, upon the oaken rooms, was grand,

And stood like a gem on velvet,
Like a radiance in some proximity to all the gods,
In reflection of a priestly calling,
And all the world turned towards me then.

(1978)

Silent in Ourselves

We are silent in ourselves,
As if accustomed to the dark,
And hardest to be penetrated,
Lie in this deepest space.

And none to know, the quality of us,
A seeming century of fill
We build around, to hold ourselves,
And appear as told what we are supposed to be.

And all the word seem sane,
Until the senses come to life
When they are at a night of wild release,
And other senses hold.

Who knows the words we could not speak,
Becoming spaces round us that we cannot break
Like unvisible surroundings,
Like walls upon our stones to walls,
No century could move.

(1979)

As if at Poem

As if at poem we stopped to look,
As if the stopping cared,
That it was raised to such a Glory,
And we were capable

To vision what we longed to see,
And it was not too late,
That we still dreamed, and had the memory,
That we were royalty,

And coaches were in vogue, for use,
And in our Satins spread,
A grand sight, in grander Expectations,
As if some miracle!

(1973)

The Place I had Been From

I do not know the place I have been from,
I had not been there long enough,
And each day like forever comes, since then,
And there is just a wait.

And pause, almost as similar to pain,
Except no feeling come, except in memory,
That is the parent of all agony,
That we are still, in time,
And rage goes on around me like a storm.

And to this place I have been from,
I gird my heritage like destiny
In all I am, that I may vision
In the soil, and grow through stalks of forest
In myself, to bloom a green society.

And each day will be all I know,
Each molecule of land a strength for me,
To simplify this age, that where I am
Shall be each thought of peace.

(1979)

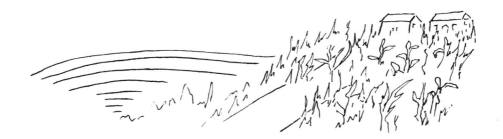

The Knowing Comes

The knowing comes with insistent need,
Each time this dream extend itself,
Like vision, closer than we would have looked,
Had we remained awake.

There is no greater than the self,
Our eyes extend within to black,
Where boundary begins in instants,
And daylight, liability.

And just beyond the range of seeing,
A vision not restricted to any form,
Comes new sight, out of the fragments
That we knew as life,
In a dimension just beyond belief.

(1979)

Selves

Our selves break into selves each pain,
And leave us fracturing,
Embodied into ghostly children,
They come to us,
Some solitude, or quiet, in the night.

Nothing there we could have said,
That would have sent the ache some other way,
We try to stabilize in regularity,
And by worn habit, face the day.

(1979)

For Self

I care for self,
As oceans do for land,
Some continuity of boundary
Where the one may start, or end.

The self is sometimes like a hold
That grasp me when I think of it,
Body like a thump to darkness,
When we land upon a form.

And I am silent,
The raging round me come
In pointed vastness, like a sound to vibration seek
To make it all the loud.

And my life comes dedicated to the still,
Where there is solitude like space,
And I may rush me all in instants,
To listen at the air for some familiar society,
Which comes like vapor in a darkened hush.

(1979)

Beyond the Care

Now, beyond the care of move,
I spin my eider things in silent ecstasy,
That in my destiny I am as free as wait,
To hold eternity.

Yet there is, ingrown, like a past,
Some urge now to be grand,
Some careful salutation of the mystery to behold,
To move in high society.

To gain some pledge, some holding
That I can on it depend,
Some payment for the agony or bliss,
But freedom, like a word
You could not have, but its act,
Come to me in a calm remembrance of truth.

(1979)

Without the Feel

It is like agony without the feel,
Some dull, compressed experience,
Unable to expose a symptom,
That body could apply a cure.

Like nothing you know of,
No sound, a silence like a touch
We could not think to place in circumstance,
And put a thought upon.

It is the passing of a day,
We held our breath, to last,
Chained by the invisibility of our chains,
That link elusive where we do not know.

Except, they shall not outlive us in this age,
We shall rot past the boundaries of self, and time,
And vision all without the constraining, finally,
When we are brave to release our deepest inner need.

(1979)

Like the Wind

It is like wind, this urge I know,
That is of a different thing than act,
We may not move upon it,
Or touch it like remnants of an age.

It is what ages are made of,
Upon the vision of society
When it is grand,
And moves like destiny in form.

We may contain it while we pause,
Deep in our nature, like suspended animation,
To stop the movement that we know
And wonder at the breadth of it.

Yet we are foreign to the mystic thing,
And beauty like a scent is lost in our thought,
We cannot comprehend the forces
That come around us like a hush.

(1979)

Other Things

There is a source I cannot say,
Although it has been life within,
And have been soul to it
Since I have known myself to be.

It is like something vaporous,
As air, though bodies are familiar with its sustenance,
And the lack of it,
And the never having known it to be not.

And it conditions me to simple things,
Like what the earth has done,
Her voices in the ground,
That plants associate to grow.

And in them, there is secret of ourselves,
That brain does not express,
A longing to be sensitive to other things
That seasons are made of.

(1979)

No Words to Tell

It would take all of rhetoric to say,
Except there are no words to tell
That we are crushed internally,
And balm too thick to penetrate.

The sinews function till the last,
The senses come at regularity,
And there, no notice of the cooling solitude,
That mark as a stamp on the ruined thing.

No lens could focus on the place,
No memory remember where it was,
Except somehow each echo of an aching sound,
Upon a seeming, empty plane,
So complete the loss.

We do not dream again, once it is gone,
The vision in us soon replace to normalcy,
And we are left as following
A feel we could not ever touch.

(1979)

There is a Fear

There is a fear that come like stone,
Into the organs flow like blood,
And harden there, we sense the weight
As slowly, as we stiffen to the thing.

It is not anything we know,
The symptom does not hold the sense,
Like pain, we cannot judge the bite,
And linger helpless bound.

It come like it has always been,
Like age when we no longer feel, as young,
And is as like a magnitude of life,
Each moment lengthened out.

It is because we do not know,
Like sounds upon a dark at still,
Depend upon imaginings of senses,
That terrorize the sound.

(1979)

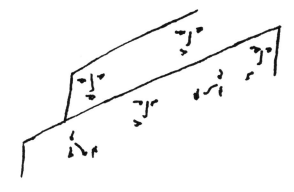

Sobriety

I am as silent to this life,
As it is still to me.
A foreigner within the workings,
I look out uncomprehendingly.

I would be all I am, at gem,
And ancient lace, all locked away,
Hidden with my sense of being,
Stationed as I am, this day.

So clocks are wound,
And hems are done,
And we are set to be,
This century, at sobriety.

(1979)

By Life

I am courted by life,
Its form come, pausing,
To me, once within a while.
And I am bound to it,

To wait, until the thing desire me,
Like gowns I think to wear,
And put us on in public fashion,
Or, out of date, in solitude.

The Life

The life is done, its silent space,
Go out like candles that we light,
Into some distant time, like layers,
Of the thing we call ourselves.

Into some distant happening,
Where we for all the world would other be,
And for it have extended,
Into ends of age for payment, for the life.

(1979)

This Clime

The clock hands have gone still,
This clime is where silence pass for comfort,
Into vagrant dreams of that better place,
Where the bounty pass for change.

And we are left, who do not form
Into this makeshift century,
Some variety of sterile passing
To the bold sobriety of need.

(1979)

Stiff Invisibility

I lift a vision at the lover
That never came to me,
That stood in separate places, distant,
While I followed in

To other worlds, more soft or dim.
With taste for such a sight as they,
Spent all my links of hour, spreading
Like a fan of ebon feathers on my face.

And I felt blackness like a hug in dark,
Like memory in still,
The feeling came, so massive
It blanketed the light like some eclipse.

Come now, be kind to me, special place,
There is no spot amid the living,
Steeped in bright, that I might stand upon,
And think some where belong.

Just silent here, the brass landscape
Surrounding me, thump into all edge
Of my desire, and melt me into
The blast of stiff invisibility.

(1979)

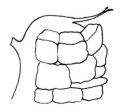

This Secret

As if the brain had loosed itself,
And memories came down
Amidst the folds of heaviness,
And then a silence came,

And then a ticking in the dark,
As slow as clocks unwound,
Into my body piled in numbers,
And to the lips began

A choking, and a laughter caught,
Like gasps from deeper pain,
A monster down in wells of deepness,
With agonies in chains.

And like my body was a voice,
He bubble into scream,
And shake me till my thoughts are only
Particles of him.

And since then, seek some less,
For knowing deep within,
A secret of my life is waiting,
For me to go with him.

(1979)

At Age

The decay grow overwhelming at age,
Its constancy of loss become
A firmament, familiar as that once,
When it was young.

In some blur of habitat and form,
Now stationed in darkened solitude,
The unexpected solidarity of silence
Gives some oasis to the blinded thing.

(1981)

Station in the Mind

There is a station in the mind
We come to suddenly at dark,
Its still bound movement
Unrecognizable to sense,

Who qualifies and quantifies the source,
To regulate, to disseminate,
Recorded in the fashions of society
To give the being form.

A Place

There is a place the mind knows
When it is past a thought,
Single station, easy to attain,
For momentary pause.

It is not built of stone, or wood,
Not finished at a hill,
Not inhabited by sense,
Formless, still.

Yet regulates the fleshy self,
Its warm desire known
By pushing past a smug sobriety,
Into depths of mad roars,
Tight behind the conscious veil.

(1981)

Good and Glorious

If I were good and glorious,
Upon a pretty hill,
Substantial in my claim of Being,
As fortune, will,

I would excuse a century,
And pardon all the foes,
And grant, immortal, to the being,
Where Heaven, grows.

And be a paramour, of Grand,
And on my Circumstance,
Plant daffodil, and fountain,
And tip my fill.

And sky would hold me, as a Dear,
And land, my breeding place,
Would spread its quiet field, upon me,
And ocean spreading near.

And I would fly, as good and glory,
And shriek, eternity,
To beauty, diamond, and perfection,
And die in grace.

(1973)

Finally They had Known

Finally they had known,
And somehow all within,
A loosening, as if they
Sensed the greatness

That would take them, wrapped,
Protected in the arms
Of glory, did not come
For them.

And so a shattering of the spirit
Of all the innocence they kept, imploded,
Until a silence settled,
Where there had been hope.

(1981)

An Ancient Orifice

An ancient orifice awake,
Its stone lips moving on the wet
We call unconsciousness,
And cause a dull urge ache,

That leak through consciousness,
Like memory we did not mean to hold,
Having been so long beyond
The terror form.

It come as silence, monster thing,
Whose soundless probing, darklike,
Comfortless attack, condemn the bearer
To the restlessness.

Cold stiffening to be touched by it,
Its claws rest upon ourselves,
As defineless as a fear without some light,
To gauge the pace of safety,
When there is a sound.

(1982)

The Self Returns

The self returns to simple ways
When fashion reach too high,
To step, in homemade fabrication,
Not daring to expose familiarity

With beings dipped in unexhausting luxuries,
In forms of satisfaction
That we had discovered, once,
Upon dim shores, some ancient

Form posing silently, tight in plated
Silks, as if an age had gone
To form the momentary permanence
Of then.

We did not belong there,
The foreign separate from us,
Too distant to extend our shyest
Once hope then upon.

The ache of belonging unsatisfied,
Our gossamered layered state of needing,
Hardly useful to demand
A caring in such bold society.

(1982)

The Forms are Ancient – 1

The forms are ancient where I am,
Survivors of a century,
Unchanged, as if their being turn
Beyond decay from hands,

That bound them with a tug.
The dusty condition out of style,
And stonefast put away, as if their
Being had lagged upon awakening,

And I was moving into light,
Internal engines said, my speed,
Some cleaner for the lack of dream,
Simplicity in bright activity.

So, from a silent calm,
This life emerge.
Some heavy movement round my being, quickening at pace,
And the beating of the day go on.

(1981)

The Forms are Ancient – 2

The forms are ancient where I am,
Survivors of a century,
Unchanged as if their being turn
Beyond decay from time,

That surround them with a haze,
Their stonelike conditions silent,
And dark, as if entombed
Into a century of night.

And I was moving into light,
The engines said, my speed
Some cleaner for the lack of else,
Simplicity in activity.

And yet a calm return, like burdened memory,
The forms continue as before,
Some heavy shadow round my fragile form,
And the beating of the day go out.

Despair at Knowledge

To me it seems of life, is Done,
And lay my tutored self soft down,
Despaired at knowledge, in its binding,
To use it as a goal.

The books are done, now, and all is full,
And I, for self, in fear,
Return to learners, in beginning,
Incapable, and weak.

And stumble over tiny words,
Who used to mean a thing,
Now out of context, scream infinity,
And throw their penciled forms, to giant size,

And rage my brain to tiredness,
Unfit, it reels at pain,
With greatness, boundless, locked at meaning,
And nothing but the word, to say.

(1973)

This Stilled Place - 1

To this stilled place I come,
For what cannot be found in bold activity,
No movement forward bring desire,
But stark simplicity

Arranges the forms,
There in thoughts of once ago
That beam forever to a need
Is vast as centuries.

I catalogue which day began my journey
Toward the thing,
Just beyond the bright tomorrow,
To return to childlike play.

The moment that my feet alight,
My tongue upon a gladdened sound,
Go sifting towards a quiet
Where the robes for god put on.

This Stilled Place - 2

To this stilled place I come,
Which cannot be found in light,
No sensibility in reason,
No stark conformity

Arranges the form there,
But thought of once ago,
That beam, conditioned to a need,
As vast as century.

I catalogue, which day directed me
Toward the thing, enlivened
Just beyond the fate my sires spent
Stumbling out their lives.

The moment that my feet were still,
My tongue upon a page,
I sifted towards a quiet
Where the robes of God put on.

(1981)

A Substance

There is a substance, made of air,
Particled in sense, and brought to form
By some connection,
Of the synapse of the self.

Some dim time when the form is still,
Its stone eyes light, and move
Across this being, like a touch,
And we become aware of it.

As if brought to consciousness, just that time,
Go searching what in memory
Has created it,
Or thoughtless, let the monster in.

It inward step, some creature
Striving to be reborn again,
We arch into the pain of it,
And silent, touch its damp, cold form,

Until it goes, and like awakening,
Return to a home,
Familiarize in touch with articles
Of present, holding us in place.

(1982)

There is a Destiny

There is a destiny in the self,
Constructed of material and air,
And registry of memory of bumping towards
Some stable mystery called need.

We bring a consciousness to it,
We long to form the substance of the thing,
As if there was no finish,
To the sense of being that we build.

It continually grows within, as if the thing
Fed easily on invisibles,
And yearns some primal push
Towards the communion

With another thing, some recognition
That the creature yearns to join together at
Some point, some still addition
Into the life we have evolved.

A Memory of Need

A memory of need contain a special quality,
Without a journey into light,
As if we were remembering some once ago
Beyond the demolition of the place, to now.

We had thought the manse so greater than ourself,
Its palace hall interior, command,
Tall regiment of form, their fashion,
Envy and desire to be had.

(1982)

This Form

We do not recognize this form,
In light, it seems the dark within
Does not illumine with a day,
Or even comfort in a similarity to night.

It is a different blindness
Than be cured by sun,
And so we reach from dark into a dark,
And linger for a while,
And go back to the silence
We had wakened from.

We Linger Past the Waiting

We linger past the waiting, for a thing,
Some noble venture to have been so faithful
To a thought of home, when there was none,
And we were unprepared to face infinity
Without a habitat.

And yet walked into our silent fate,
With just an apron pushed against
The terror, past our room,
For there no longer was a difference to be there.

And since that day we carry all the universe
We know, girded soft along,
Some road to spend the still moments
Out, till we are past all consciousness.

(1984)

The Place Been From

We do not know the place been from,
It must have been a greater thing
Than we aspired to, in this consciousness,
Now dull, in some dark space of life.

To face the self, uneasily,
A burden in the present form,
That must have had potentialities,
Beyond our simple thought.

That must have had a legacy,
A sweet inheritance, some gift,
Or talent, easy to delight,
To hold the age, enthralled.

To be so now, unsteadily,
At age, to drift, as if no mooring
Could hold this foreigner,
Not meant for such a shoddy paradise.

Like Some Dim Beast

There is a silence at the mind,
Like some dim beast, now accustomed
To a foreign habitat of cage,
Remain unmoving, where once paced

Skillfully the form of his estate.
As if the waiting formed anew,
Into some pattern of the brain,
Where he no longer found

External stimulation past air, and
Into depths along the movements
Of some memory, or soft
Beating in the form,

Become the only regulation
That he focus on,
To hold himself at station,
At this final place he has come to.

(1984)

The Maiden

The maiden finally puts away her wait,
The day is not so long,
The room is silent as her step,
And to the thought of gone.

She marks, as smoothing at her hair,
It was not for a loss to go,
She could not hold the thing
That came to everyone but her.

That settled like an evening snow,
That covered like an eider gown,
That shone like diamond palaces,
But to her, only felt like cold.

(1994)

Life Station

In our final, life station,
We must choose carefully the gown,
For cannot naked be, the
Climate is too chilly for such luxury

Of naked celebration, that some native
Knew, before he was committed
To the station of the roar,
Of some society.

We were all pinks and yellows once,
When we were just so young,
It did not matter, for the covering
Only enhanced the softness of the cheek,

And careless brow. It was a sweet addition
To be draped in gauze, not now,
The blood does not rush up so high,
And pallor does not match the day.

There, at the other end of this long
Consciousness, lie velvets hanging
Full, their folds inviting to
Enwrap the weakened form in deep maroons,
And midnight blue.

And lastly a primal longing to have known,
What it would have been like to crouch
Intently by a fire, covered only
By the dust our nature blew.

(1996)

A Final Show

There is a final show we must put on,
It is not difficult to do,
To glean from the scripts
And versions, we have played, that long ago.

For one last cameo of act,
The heart still has not lost its hope,
The play, like wooden boys grow real,
The hope for magic, hope for feel.

And so, one last time for the dream
The gods have loaned us,
Who cannot bear to see us so alone,
Upon the naked plains we live.

We don the golden Inca mask,
Its jade eyes glistening in amber light,
And step upon that platform,
Raised, that we may come in view.

And listen for our cue, to speak,
To that sacrificial lover cast into the role,
Who sways slightly, bound raw before us,
We reach out, as we have been trained,

And say the words which we have learned,
Enfold our bloody embrace in this one scene.
Perhaps it is dramatic, or a comedy,
But cannot tell the difference,

(Continued)

Because the ending seems the same,
But some sweet variety
To this stiff posture, cunning role of life,
Draws us to this closing act, sublime.

And we imagine such a joy
As we raise the beating heart of sacrifice,
Its warmth a momentary thrill
To feel the life it once contained.

(1996)

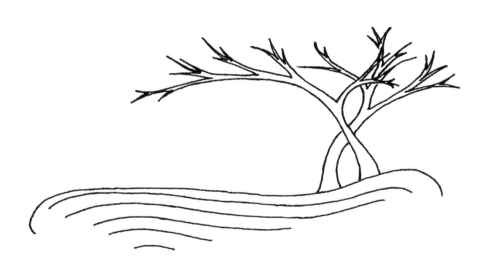

New England

I am New England born,
Where stone walls met the sea,
Of macintosh, and pasture, and meadow,
Of clapboard, and pine, of fir.

Where garden ran along the stone,
In lilac, lily of the valley,
And into wood, pink lady slippers,
On moss, and fern.

And in silence grew, a silent place
To grow, for we were self contained
There, old when young, whose fire passion
Never broke the surface of ourselves.

You would not know the place been from,
It is no longer in the world,
Which timeless dwelling was erased,
When worldly things found voice.

And no one now believes in still,
The forest temples cut away,
They did not find the soul of our life within,
When they dissected in the light.

(1998)

So Small a Freight

I begged for reprimand, of Day,
I could not bear the light,
Centuries unthought of, Marching,
Upon so small a freight.

There only was enough, to Eat,
And moments tragedy,
A tatted sail upon a post,
And I.

Princes beat the shore with Gold,
A general turned the sky,
Only fortitude of Holy,
Only Greatness, here!

A Silence

There is a silence in the stillness
Only those can know,
Who are not children of the world they live,
Nor passenger of this strange voyage,
We call life.

Some orphans of the firmament,
Who, strange upon the land do walk,
In danger that they be exposed,
In fear they shall be ravaged by a multitude.

Yet are not even noticed by the passersby,
And sink a fathom lower than the hunted beast,
Who link the chain of some necessity,
To eat a life in hunger, to preserve themselves.

They are lost, for there will never be
A time when they are heard,
When ears could notice such a thing,
Nor feel the press of lips without the teeth,
Nor feel a touch, without the slap,
And are pushed aside
Like rubble of past century.

(1998)

I Call

I hold pretentious as the Bee,
Who girds a flower sill,
And opens in the air, her Nectar,
And dips his fill.

And all that hear are petal things,
Who think it was the Wind,
And sigh as they are courted, being
Beauties, by some tufting air.

I call as if I were a pearl,
Shimmering in Sea,
Just dropped by Mollusk in his grave,
And drowned in sinking mire.

To be saved, to climb a neck in light,
To smooth on Velvet plush,
To feel the bounty of a Station,
And keep, forgotten, Out.

But rest unheard, and as a Flake,
Descend to whiter Still,
Just noticed by the blast of Nature,
Who crushes as she will.

(1973)

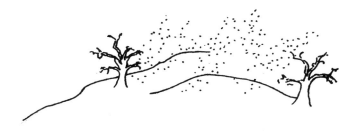

I Wished

I wished, that I could be as Great
As those who, come to Know,
And play at magic things, uncovered,
Instilled magnificence.

Order up the Solar system,
And mark it, studied, down,
Simplifying bold intention,
Standing, world to World!

And heaven, gold, and glazed Embalm,
Stately rows of view,
I wished that I, could, be the Number,
Chosen of the few.

The Burden

It is the burden of my Gown
That makes me saddest, now,
As if I had to please a Legion,
And smile throughout the town.

And stand apart, my silent fate,
And seem congenial,
And linger past the day, in waiting,
As if some moment come

To take me in, some sacrament,
To raise me in the air,
Like mystic vision sanctity,
Like glory, everywhere!

(1973)

Future Now

My future is now.
There is no more to hold, or give,
There is not that retentive nature to preserve,
There is not that being to become.

Rejoice with me then, cold,
Which is not powered by engines to be warm,
Which is not compromised by comforting,
And does not need acceptance to exist.

Ache in me then, heat,
Which burns though I am not consumed,
Which lights though I need not see,
For I am you, and that

Which once was outside of me,
Is no longer out of reach,
Becomes in me itself again
And we are ever one.

Denied, though whole,
Rejected, though firm, disallowed,
Though taking all that has been,
And my being revives
As does the Phoenix renewed.

(1998)

Voiceless Children

It is enough to have been saved,
The victims of a wreck report,
For there is hope again
For comfort in the parlors of their lives,
And fresh continuation of themselves.

For it was just a careless loss of altitude,
Or leak, or unexpected circumstance,
Which had exposed them to misfortune,
None could have predicted to have been.

Yet there is still another loss that comes.
No damage for the saviors to inspect,
Is visible, no wound to bind,
No mar of face or disarrangement
Of the style they wear.

It is interior, elusive to the cutting blade,
Or powders ground for narcotic properties,
Cannot apply themselves, it, mutant, lies
Transforming now, into an anger, or
A blackness of a shutting down of sense.

It is a greatest secret that I know.
In its slimed grasp have been,
The terror to the innocent,
Burning pyre bright, the violence that consumes,

And we cannot escape it, though we run.
And time is stopped,
And they inject their madness
Through cold ravaging of the helpless form.

(continued)

We, once light simplicity,
Now take on this yoke,
And blinder, and feel weight that Atlas,
Timeless man, alone, could sympathize.

(1998)

The Salmon Bell

I hear the salmon bell in me,
That has been heard in rarity.
An odd, magnetic pull to home,
I see it, splintered like an ancient bone,
That had a history of sorts,
That one day must have had a place,
Forgotten now, lies testament of some dim past.
The story, simple pages tell, of life
To hunger, shelter, rest, and die.
Yet I have heard the bell, and I,
Have been to what had been a home,
That was not home, a terror place,
To run, as orphans must in mind,
To anywhere, there, passing time.
Or immigrant whose box, or book,
He carried as schematic, to remind,
Yet cannot find an interest from his family,
Who does not want the memory,
They see no old one by a cottage door,
Now in a land of more and more.
Whose price is change, until the landscape
Must remove, the possibility of spawn
Is gone, to roe and caviar.
But yet I hear the salmon bell in me,
That sounds a voice of destiny,
That says, oh come to me,
Despite the ruined path, be free.

(1999)

Hungry Know

Waiting is all the hungry know,
Who do not fill on food,
Who eat until their senses crumble,
Yet are not satisfied.

Who have a pit beneath themselves,
Till Chinas are in view,
And nothing to expel their terror,
Of the deepening.

      (1999)

Ourselves to Selves

The reach amid ourselves to selves,
Is more silent, the closer to a deeper need express,
As if the dream-like station
Formed, before ability of word.

      (1981)

We Have Left Sobriety

Though I have left sobriety,
It lingers, pale self unable to mount
The old lover, becomes spectral,
In its failed ability to unite.

I am far away from such bland posing,
Such concentration of detailed niceties,
That once ago induced me
To be pleasant in.

That tract of self propriety is done.
There is no caring to be part
Of what no longer feels,
Does not warm when cold internals

Are in need of touch,
The one thing I could not self provide.
The one desire to be needed,
Was there not possible to have.

It was what put me in these silent rooms,
To loosen the gown of that society,
It slips down, to let my nakedness
Reflect the primal form I have exposed.

(2002)

Sobriety Comes

Sobriety comes like a push
Some morning past inebriation,
Or desire satisfied, or pain spent,
Or falling in the wood.

Suddenly pitched to inch forms
That we hardly felt,
Their stable forms familiar
To an ancient oak or beast,

Of forest life, now shuddered
At rest, we sharpen on that
Form reality, and pause from nearly
Having pitched into some dark.

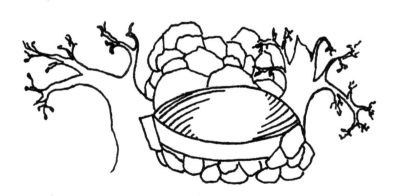

My Muse

Past

2. Past

Poem Number One

Alone give me waterfalls,
To sit on their brim,
Looking over the times to go,
Replacing those gone by,
And dream that once alone are we,
With all these things,
My memory, and me.

(1966)

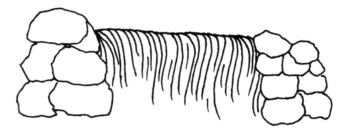

The Orbs are Gone

The orbs are gone that turned to gold,
The memory is dim,
The lands that fortune coveted,
Are sold into the sea.

The diamonds are all plate this year,
And shining, are as dull
As graves where beings lie awakened
By the news of fail.

Soon their weariness is lifted some,
Their eyes begin to see,
The stones that hold them are unhinging
As they rise to come.

And all the air is still as black,
And all the mind aware,
Scream innocent, as they remember
Who had buried them.

And to him make their tired way,
And scream into his brain,
Till he is maddened by their sorrow,
And joins them in their death.

(1976)

So Long We Waited

So long we waited at the door.
It seems its oakness vast within,
Enwrapt us in a hardlike substance,
And everything was silent there.

And every tick would almost stop,
And every feeling stretch,
Like arrows to our brain in hungering
For targets to be in.

And how our memories return,
We almost thought as child,
And hum some almost tune against the quiet,
And think how grand we must have stood.

How difficult the solitude.
Its mightiness always the biggest thing we know,
And like some iron pushed into us,
We slowly weight so much,
Then all forget how light we were.

(1976)

Just One More Time

Just one more time, we try
The tired fashion gown around us,
Just to feel its memory, bodice of our once agos,
Easy to put on.

And stand amid the hidden room,
And feel the silk renew,
Our slippers treading now in palace,
Our fingers clutching pearl.

Our standard bearers form anew,
Each dream as possible as be,
And we are prating yes to heaven,
And in procession go.

The banquets are prepared for us,
And through the courtyards step,
To weddings in our mind and body,
And our gentleman,

Who waits not far away for bliss,
We bring in endless bowls,
And to him, beautiful, are readying,
In magical delight.

(1976)

Suddenly the Moments Come

Suddenly the moments come
And linger specially,
That seem as if the kingdom had returned,
And we could wear a crown.

And there could be a chance again,
That slippered on glazed floors,
We might attain the majesty,
We might achieve the place.

And turn our backs to dull concern,
The goddess at high,
Return the forests to our liking,
Revive the burned estate.

But memories build their terror huts
And rage into the air,
And breed some inability to move,
And tear at all the world.

And then I cling to my escape,
The airs more gentle there,
Like beast upon a wood,
Rush blindly to the wild familiarity of nature glen,
And slip into my den.

(1978)

Dignity of Despair

The sweetest wine is mellow, there,
The dignity of despair,
Unhooks her robes of quietness,
Fermenting, everywhere.

Where I had been, another day,
Had come upon the green,
At summer's lasting, now in focus,
From a distant mien.

A feeling, so that moments bend,
Into the place of then,
Surround the present at its stillness,
In colors, and smell, of when.

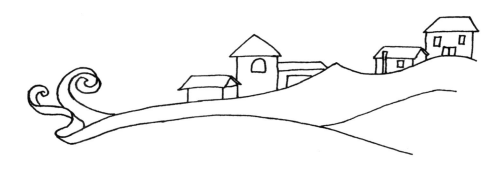

The Hardest Work

The hardest work is what's most done,
And left there little room,
To put in pleasant, modern, things,
To help a mind grow on.

The sorrow comes, a constant wind,
Expected, and most known,
Unaccustomed to be leaving,
Unexpected, to be gone.

She fills with dust, she scrubs the past,
She shines a rusty blade,
And touches where it used to sever,
Discovered by a rotted scar.

The paths are cold, and laden under,
By memories, too hard to lift,
So stay to be somehow uncovered,
As if they'd never gone, to rest.

(1969)

The Conquered Wreck

So unsuspecting, from a desert
Have come into the dust,
And parch my lips that crack for air,
And stumble where I lay.
How better off are old survivors
Still upon the conquered wreck.

From the Forest

From the forest, I have been,
But almost, don't recall
Places where the trees are royal,
And land wears Softest things.

I'm of the wood, haven't you heard?
I'm calling everywhere,
Telling from the rooftops,
And down into the towns.

Of this, so bold alliance,
I had at child, and then,
From some unspoken mystery,
Can only remember, when.

(1973)

Once Ago

Once ago there was a wood,
And in it Gentle were the things,
And time stood dignified in Station,
Pausing everything.

And I was free, and Roamed at land,
And knew the daffodil,
And where the lady slipper Prospered,
And where the goldenrod.

And how the moments lingered there,
It seemed eternity,
That I was part of such a bounty,
That I could simply be.

(1973)

A Last Remembrance

I am dull and sweet, and to no one Prosper,
In this land of might have been,
My dreams are ever bound in dungeons,
And to them, colored leaves and grass, I send.

Even here, I am not grand
Among the ruined and the lost,
As if some crown I could not hide,
Stood just too Royal,
And I too weak to hold it long,
And time, just footing to exist,
And mercy, angel grace, unnecessary here.

I miss them, as I fade for Darkness,
And in demise take all the memory
I can hold, and kiss its dusty lip,
A last remembrance.

(1973)

Accustomed

I am accustomed to the grave,
And glory, and better been,
And of the world, know little of her,
Though she, as ancient as myself.

Am ever awed each morning day,
That I, still upon, do thrive, though little
In such a foreign place, and habitat,
And language out of style, for me.

And each old sight, is ever new,
And each remembrance, a breath,
As if it never went to once ago,
And each fresh time, to stun me down.

(1973)

Sophisticate

Sophisticate of dismal things,
I faint each moment by,
And beauty fathom, in its passing,
Past I.

Of once ago, I try to reach,
As if at nature, gained the way
To call in dead leaves to life, that linger,
And smell their sweetest embrace.

(1973)

Milkweeds

I, and nature, consecrate
Additions to the wind,
Settling in mounds of valley,
Vagabonds of tuft.

Ballerina evening gowns,
A dozen ladies' things,
Dancing to the autumn forest,
In silver diadems.

Where ever are the folk,
Tossing at the breeze,
There, open spaces in the moss,
To let the fainting milkweeds, in,

And cover up their lighted stay,
Bear down the pleated folds,
Melt the unsuspecting floaters,
To memory, and me.

(1974)

Hopeless Stilled

The black sky on its edge,
I faint in memory,
Homeless to belonging,
Unexplainable to my lack of care.

That house is burned,
The land is sold,
The family is dead, but me.
The albums of my testament

Are scattered in a grave somewhere,
And I am hopeless stilled.
Inheritance at lip is sealed,
I dare not scream the loss,

But cover round my softened body,
The blankets of despair,
And linger in my bed this season,
And dream of houses otherwhere.

(1975)

Somewhere in the Brain

Somewhere in the brain I stopped to be,
And visit with the graves, such centuries
It seems ago the children lain there,
And their memories descended to myself,
Of wondering why they had died,
And if their little forms were gently laid,
Or were forgotten on this stretch of ancient cold,
Where there is solitude.
So still this dim enfolds itself in night,
And there is never reason for the day,
And all the trees forget to grow, and grasses
Gray and slick with rotting damp,
Where they, immortal, grasp the hidden earth
In clutches, keeping silent as I touch the hidden forms,
That lie so ever down.

(1975)

No Paradise to Try

The house is rotted at the hill,
The family bones are dry
Beneath the lilac, where a sunken plot
Is left, no paradise to try.

No letters from the land of gone,
Their fingers quilting dust today,
Cause memory to bend an instant
Out of time, and with them long to die.

(1975)

The Dropped Past

Pained here, we think to lift
Our bruised head above the beatings,
So commonly experienced once ago,
Because we were alive.

About the dropped past, stubborn bent,
Still trying to be present in its fevered clutch
Of breath, as if it had some power
To remain so long, the memory survive.

Stiff and fragile,
We mark each moment in comparison,
To something worse that might have been,
Inductor of the present sorrow,
And progenitor of agonies.

(1975)

The Memory

It was as if the mansion burned
When I was out to sea,
Striving on a bark with fortunes sold,
For diamonds by the Orient.

And ocean smooth as glass, it seemed
Superior to land,
As casual as plush to velvet ladies,
At their fingertips.

The carpets, gone, the drawers of silk,
The oak, as dark as coal,
Ruined as I turned upon the hillside,
To the new despair.

Sisters gone, their bosoms cold,
The cellars now a tomb
For them, and me to find the fortress
Done, and hide into the memory.

(1975)

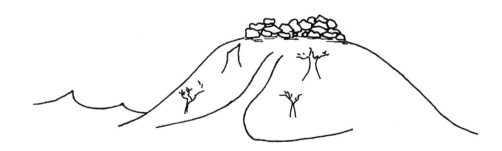

Kneeling at my Room

Kneeling at my room, I touch the wall,
To wonder how it stand so well,
So long around me as I cling in thought
Of sight, when there were windows here.

And I would sit each day to look
Out at the forest edge, and fields,
And sustenance of sun abound,
And then occasional, an animal.

And I would almost think them in,
The carpets laden down
With mosses, and a flower, and some trees,
Intact upon the room.

And there were streams, and palaces,
Around the cupboard door,
And shaded spaces on the table,
Below the ferns in air.

And suddenly, as if a night
Spread out as big as me,
Pushed all the visions by the curtain,
And closed them out of sight.

And into me, a darkening,
A fading of the memory,
Of when there was a habitat
Of light, and, air, and free.

(1975)

Some Ancient House

Some ancient house,
Whose vast expanse, now grim,
Withstand alone on empty floors,
Yet stand as it had meant to do,
From builders' hands,
Though life within had failed its purposes.

There I lie, last descendant
Of a foreign breed, who lingered
Past the age that bred my sensibility,
That formed my stiff, unyielding form.

Am no longer sentient to worldly thing,
To pose among the jocund crowd
Of blindered, shapeless specters,
Moving towards their opened tombs.

I am upon that last, decaying ark,
That in some hidden wood, stood faded
As the century that passed beyond its silent memory,
That left it as a final artifact, of me.

(1975)

Twilight Notions

Like twilight notions and moon most full,
Upon the heather, to some drunken Child,
I think this life in contrast to another,
Be so full of dreams, spun once ago.

Till to the harvest place, it find no vegetable
Quite from its planting, faint seeds rotted
In the hidden soil, so promised on that
Fertile day, their bounty bear.

And so as if I had it lived,
This life infuriates my better sensibility
To shuck it off, and have the better been,
That first all blinded season,

Unbeknown to failure when I lived,
That way, where touch, the clearest thing,
Would crystal up the World,
And dreams crack brittle
On their phony continent.

(1975)

As If

As if the biggest ocean shrunk
Into me like a sponge,
And all my skin had held it in,
And all the fishes squeezed.

And when I breathed, the slowness dared
To move the air within,
And just a drop would trickle outwards,
And I would look the same.

And gird my apron like before,
And shut the doors at day,
And strive my little being round
To hold the sorrow in.

And wonder if I dare to gasp
And flood the monster world,
Or hide and hope it never passes
With another sea.

(1976)

To Memory

We do not know the loss, till life
Turns inward like a hush,
And sits to live in majesty
With what we have become.

Our shabby rooms are hidden till that time,
No notice that there had been else,
And we go forward in activity,
Of change that seem to regulate so well.

There is no accounting till the last,
All seem to turn by will,
Till some turn childlike, and they are ancient
As perennials.

No one knows the time it takes,
It is like when we feel the first,
That we have turned our eyes to memory,
And find ourselves in peace.

(1979)

The Solitary Dark

It is as if I have been to doom,
The terror house come gentle,
Like it did not scare the child,
Since he had been to kingdoms of the stuff.

And all the night was like a pause,
Its dim vision as familiar as the self
He know now well,
Each space some cause from silence,

Almost hidden in the still.
Yet scream a chanting voice, like pasts
Whose agonies a memory contain,
And stand the night apace as timeless been.

I am executor of this state,
To think the ghost-like things
Could swell the universes from their hold,
And hurl eternally upon the solitary dark.

(1979)

It Came More Gentle In

As if I could not bear the thing,
It came more gentle in,
As pause between the pain,
Some narcotic allow.

It come as soft as eider down,
Like a tap down in the door,
Where we are silentest,
Away from all the louding things.

It did not have a word to say,
Too big, I think, upon the lips
Of such a one to speak,
Just form, and me.

And then it was like in the brain,
A knowing come, as if some ago,
Remembered why it was,
Why still upon a need,

And rallied in the thought, some touch,
Of being of what it was,
And reached out to the thing, all knowing,
And then it faded out.

(1979)

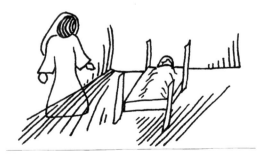

The Condition

This state is like a haze to me,
I cannot speak its name or place,
Or put the memory in pattern
That brought me to the thing.

It is a fear as well I know,
Like sensibility at pause,
When all the mind is racing to a thing
To fathom its danger, or disease.

And I am further past the cause of it,
That to still live at consciousness
Does all depend
On being distant from the thing.

Into my tomblike mind
I record this condition, like pieces
Of an art of faces,
That must have fit some Stygian creatures
To be so monstrous.

(1981)

At the Tip of Sense

At the tip of sense, and on,
We gage, familiar at the place
Where creature come, some fission
Torn of self upon ourself.

They are limited in scope of being,
Their forms give some semblance
Of when, before, were first come to us,
To us like variation of some repeated dream.

Of some repeated dream when they had
Entered in, dark carriers of fate,
Whom we remember through the scope
Of their familiarity and feel.

They stretch inward on, symbolic recreations
Of the terror of some thought
Or happenstance, now molded down
To character of memory
We lean into, when close to having
Recreated what had crushed upon us, once.

Into the Terror House

Into the terror house awake,
As if we had not left the thing,
Its fashion familiar, from ago,
Remembering, since the once,

We first encountered what it was,
A new pain, like the first exposure
Into the flame,
Some permanence of memory.

And turn upon the shadow form,
Its constant regulation to us firm,
As if some ghostly wedding
To unite each once again.

And turn like dials to what has been,
Somehow a vision on the once agos,
Collected brittle, lifeless, in a clarity,
We ache so, as it revive.

An Older Sound

I strive to an older sound, than now,
The passing of a thing, like fossil,
Hardens into essence of the being,
Great stones to sink into me, to give me form.

Without the metamorphosis of death,
I can align the boundary of once,
And fill old lungs with then,
And breathe the clearer air of them.

Simplicity of antique fashion that I wear,
Easy to put on,
The memory without the lifetime
It required, to be consciousness.

And to the ages come,
Somehow some quality amid the ancient forms,
Expose old century anew,
To those who fit these sires' gowns.

The Final Loss

We do not know the final loss,
Till gone far past the memory,
As if again upon the moment,
Having circled in our age

Upon the thing again, we knew.
We are different in the second quest,
Our older form not innocently hopeful, to reach out,
And not the openess.

And not the simple trust, that when
We had been there,
Seemed biggest to our form, could manage,
Daring as we stood.

Somehow the bold necessity
Go out the second time,
We reach into the same unknowing,
With such a weariness.

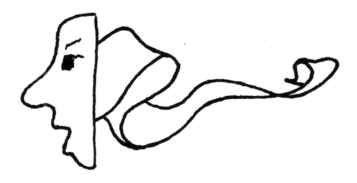

Since that Moment

Since that moment, and before,
Are like some different lives,
Abruptly zeroed from the once ago
To after it had been.

No marker to the visible,
No pediment of sight,
To happeners upon the incident,
They, in their own ability,

Prepare to some faint destiny,
While we, ablaze, that terror happening
Divide the universe for us,
Till forever, now.

Upon the spot, as time goes out of date,
We gaze as it is always then,
It seems the horror thing,
The millionth time relived.

The Memory of Hope

The brightest, is the memory of hope.
We still position in our room,
A place we visit silently,
As some stone artifact of once,

Whose grandsires, less of thought,
Stood firm, that century.
We glimpse as unintentional expenditure,
Their numbed expression,

Which evolve in us, a dower, an excess of need.
As if the blood expose
A bursting of staid ancestral posing,
Finally ragged here.

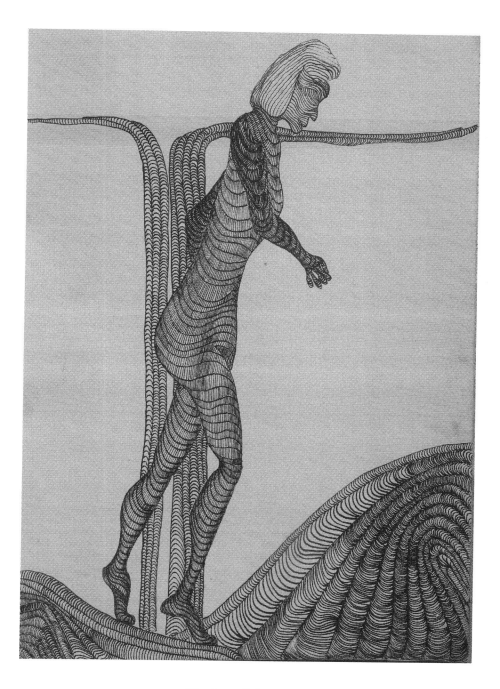

Baba Yaga

3. Death

The Hardest Things

The hardest things are easiest
To find yourself to do,
Moving into Zanzibar, or changing
Who you love the best, from some necessity.

To rearrange the stars at ease,
To check the planets down,
And leave your mansion for a hovel,
Somewhere out of town.

But what the slightest child can do
The millionth time a day,
Impossible, at each reflection,
Moving at our feet.

To tie our bonnet one last time,
And close the oaken door,
With just a look at no returning,
And down the path no more.

While everyone is on the street,
We linger vast inside,
And take eternity in moments,
To suffer centuries.

(1975)

Cold Wonder Child

Rise up, cold wonder child,
The barrens are silent and empty
Now that you are gone,
Since you have been removed from the wood.

You do not run there anymore,
Where you foraged sweet bark,
Resting at the warm sun, just past dew,
Out in familiar walks.

Black coat blending tan rushes bending,
You short time rising in me,
I would not have known what could have been,
Had you not come to me,

Now crushed out, here, not in your habitat.
This ever awareness, ever separation
From you, my natural oneness,
I bend into you

Like child memories of what I must have been.
Stark innocence once in movement,
Your soft beauty, so in death,
Absorb into my own decay, your passing.

(2002)

Riker

There is no loss, but future days,
Spent departed from the one.
Each, searing in its tepid passing,
Each dark, in light.

Cheap words do no contain it,
Not funeral etiquette for studied grief,
Not sob, weakness and shallow,
For the breath of it.

It does not contain, not condense,
Not communicate. The solitariness
Of grief is not shared.
It is not left in stone and plot.

It is the separation, daily to come,
First, like a draft felt,
Then the taking away, the endless,
Empty, forever, tedious getting through,

The going on while looking back,
The time stopped, while time go on,
The imagining at the loss, while pushed along,
The loneliness unhinged, unfathomed,
To be now, daily drowned.

(April 17, 2006)

Beloved Child

There is a grief that tries to speak,
Though words stutter within.
Language become hazed, as if at rule
Syntax change and meter sag.

What had been distant, observational,
Now pushed as if into walls, like water
Streaming into senses, closing, removing air,
In this primal depth of loss.

To communicate the ache, some habit
To express what does not express,
To act upon the painless pain
That nerve does not transmit, balm not heal,

Thought not organize, sense not reach.
None can lessen the swollen thing
That mind attempt to rule,
That it might steady and continue on.

It is the solitary task of one,
To shoulder what death has taken in moment,
To replace the solid life with spectral void,
That weights in ceaseless, formless tons.

(2006)

Zippy

I am past the light,
This speeding thing propelled at breath,
Accelerate past solar systems,
Ignite rapidity.

This form of consciousness, my vessel,
This receptor of sensation, my guide,
This storage unit of perception,
The thing that sear, like friction.

The thing that burn me in my station,
The source of my flight,
The boundless searching of my memory
Of loss, of wrenching silence,

Of what is not not here with me,
Of what has stayed behind
As I have gone on,
Gone past the sting that hurl me on,

Gone past the moment of the having,
Past the heart's desire in me,
Past the caring for this journey,
I reach back helplessly.

(2008)

This is the Day

This is the day that grief become me,
Its grey, formless mist upon me,
Its moist eyes into my eyes press,
Blocking other sight from me.

And I step anew, fresh formulation,
New character from what had been,
Gulfs from then to now in moments,
In one breath, now stilled.

In one cold flash, the changeling be,
Its inner form moulded, melted,
Into another shape without mold,
Without form, except it be,

Like lumps, like sludge, like thickness
Within. The vessel of then is gone.
The holding thing is burst,
The retaining, containing thing is gone.

And I remain, amophous thing,
Ghostly thing of what had been
So crystalline, so clear,
So bright, so burnished in my crystal form.

(2008)

There is a Holding On

There is a holding on that pass,
A caring, that decay to ground,
A passing that evolve itself
In some new form, eventually.

Slowly move, it shape, its leaden self,
It breathe again, it start,
Like some golem move,
Like some dim replacement, take its place.

And what had been, is memory,
Old station there, like antiquity,
Quaint, once place, we observe
From distances unfathomable.

From station now in life, apart,
From now to then depart,
From how and when, cannot start
To imagine what had been.

(2008)

It is the Putting On of Grief

The shriek of loss is done
That stun the outer world
Who switch and toss their vacant heads,
Who gape at agony.

The impropriety has ceased.
The wail grown hoarse,
The running stop, breath calmed,
Eye turned toward activity that come.

It is the putting on of grief.
It is the strain of its grey load
That cause the groan, the burden
Filtering on the granite dust,

That make the yell, soon spent,
And then a quiet come.
Piercing quiet to the bone,
Which magnify the emptiness without.

That expose hollow rooms,
Which had seemed filled
When there was life. When
There was such distraction,

That the life seemed in its wake
To charm the very walls
It moved along, to lighten the very breath
It shared with what it loved.

(2008)

The Silence of Loss

The silence of loss, mouths without sound
Scream inner mourning, seep within,
All now memory of what had been,
Past touch, out of reach to sensation,

That expand as if boundaries were infinity
Beyond space, to fill what had been
Within arms, that had been within
Our simple grasp, that had contained us.

That had filled us, contented us at moments,
A quiet that moved around us in circles,
Rounding us in a separate peace
That did not require to be more.

It was enough to be contained
Like planets, in our round circumference.
And now spread out, in linear expansion
Push out at the shattering of whole.

Spread out as bursting things,
Leach into the the atmosphere, an ether
Released from its exploded vial,
To scatter, expanding in gasses

Where formless shapes dissolve,
Like the essence of breath disintegrate
From the life gone out from us,
From our point of being, depart.

(2008)

There is an Ache

There is an ache like growths expand,
Like tumors press the body cavity
Till it puff out with malignant things,
Till it blast out like carcasses.

Yet live on. The disease has not infected
The inner machinery. It has not decayed
The synapse channels at the brain
That function still, like automation run.

The destruction is silent and invisible,
Microscopic to the greater form,
Incidental seeming to the senses, gleaming
Information to the being, still alive.

Still in motion past the simple death.
Appearing apart, the form move
After the incident. Continue after
The putting away of the little life,

The great being shake itself and go.
It cannot stop where the creature lay
To be forever moveless, to be still,
The being lumber forward, helplessly.

(2008)

Dark Street

This is the dark street, hidden street,
From other streets, lighted, scorched lane habitats
Where land creatures roam endlessly
In measured droves, their eyes averted.

This is deep street, silent street,
Where none pass through.
None come here. Old shadows hide
Rustic things, covered in vine.

And colorless forms rise up
As old buildings, giant forms
Of log and frame, damp things
That are the center of this street.

That contain the heart of it,
This house is the chamber of the source
Of this place, this other dwelling place
From parched beyond, lighted places

That are hidden from us here. This is
The center of the thing,
The beast source, the home of it.
The dwelling of the creature.

Here it breathes, the only sound.
Its hooves unmoving, furred paw still.
Its eyes motionless, it waits.
It waits to pierce the surface of the night.

It holds a grief we must encircle,
It stations by the dead form we must embrace,
It keeps the still form before our blinded eyes,
Until we pull it in ourselves.

(2008)

The Future Peace

What we must leave behind,
Where we must turn away,
The gentle mound along the hillside,
The slightest space, of all our care,

Must from the rise descend,
Must turn at day, to bend
Upon the moving trial of some activity,
And in the masses blend,

Who do not feel the core removed,
Who do not know the hollowed space
We leave within, the hidden, leaden veil
Upon us, the loss, the aiery gentle thing,

The slip of child, the bond of grace,
The hold of faerie touch, removed,
The parting where the senses linger,
To grow numb, all future peace.

(2008)

The Tonic

Here roar the silence of a piercing loss,
Where all internals beat a hidden sound,
What is no longer visible to sight
Because the moment passed when it had life,

When it surrounded like atmosphere,
Immersed, liquid in its suffusing energy
To fill what had lain parched in more arid times,
But now had blossomed forth in earthen paradise.

Where each thought was pleasant balm,
Where all pasts were done,
It lay in presents, each awakening
Like fresh birth in our room-sized universe.

In our slight space, won at wars,
It came, fleshing peace, ferment calm,
It nestled in, it nested on our beating warmth,
It rested like all trial was done.

(2008)

There is a Silence

There is a silence, like dust,
Where had been movement,
Where unexplained, untired activity
Had been, like motors running,

Had been unnoticed in its simplicity,
Had been an engine of smooth motion
Where each moment in seamless pattern
Revoloved, like gears, like pistons,

Moving to experience. There was
All motion that glided as oiled,
As bearinged, rolling motion,
As self contained, complete, unattached.

It was as home must be,
And contentment must contain, as peace,
As what centers, what forms whole,
What contains breath of life.

It had been what does not stand out,
What does not show, its depth of being
As bedrock to conscious experience,
As source of senses, as source of expression,

As joy to be, this wonder thing,
Who thought it could be separate?
What predict it could depart the self,
And leave a trackless, coasting, noiseless thing?

(2008)

A Letting Go

There is a letting go, at loss,
Like drowning, suffocation at the brain
That dies in portions, at connections,
Where the joining had been lain.

There is a piercing at the center,
There is a cauterizing sear
That chokes the senses as a madness,
That pulls away the thought of self.

That weakens as the storm abate,
That alter what had been, till now,
The lessening, like leaden mist descend,
To blur what had been whole.

To stain what had been very bright,
To rend the seamless eye,
Till it see where the heart had tattered,
And mar the view of day.

(2008)

Where Latitude was Dim

He asked of, why, we stopped,
Where latitude was dim,
And whether it was night, or just
Some storm, or circumstance.

And why, I could not think, to speak,
And why, I could not say,
To tell him this was home,
And we at last had come to stay,

Was more than I could then express,
This wretched hovel, bare,
Exposed the quality of our existence,
On this plane of useless care.

(1972)

A Fatal Reach

Beyond eternity, and me,
Lies an ancient sea,
And all inhabitants inside,
Were, pilgrims, before.

There were the cowslips, and the bell,
Trampled out of life,
And all the heavy feet that trod,
Lie facing toward the shore.

There is a ship that leaves, each life,
With solitary rooms,
And all the passengers that go,
Leave without the time.

Umbrellas furled, and lace,
With velvet, fills the deck.
Waiting as if the ship would go,
While the landscape pulls away.

The mottled crew, collects the passage,
Just a penny, each,
Then steers the ship into the voyage,
With a fatal reach.

(1969)

We Are Not Pages

Let us eat of death, its fetid sauce
Blanched to our taste, so disguised
To appear as life,
Creamy, blood soups, sugared over humps
Of now grey flesh.
We eat of death to sustain
Near death, not life,
We are not pages written in.
We are that which goes out
For all our powers of creating immortality,
We fail internally. Not life,
The great queen spreading eggs
Is only life death, but our shaping
To be comprehended, though we never spoke,
Retains what seeming life we had.
It is not the flashy touch that lingers,
Or sustains, or is life food.
That appearing intensity is only heat.
That appearing attraction is only
To reproduce us, because we are not life.
That, there, is bound from us,
For all our sweet fading youth, smiling.
A permanence goes on, vibrant
To what withers, what looks in
On frosted nights through stone glass,
Into life's rooms that glow, sparkle,
Because we are not inside,
And life can go fresh from us,
Though we have formed it,
May not participate.

(2003)

Stun the Void

To shriek and stun the void,
That round me creep, silent rot,
Increasing to a smell of ruin,
I fear to breathe.

And in pain, an old escape,
That drain me from my faded dreams,
And make them simple as a moment,
That will pass to other things.

To have lost eternity, and spent my future gifts,
And feel the darkness round,
A tremble lest I turn my head,
And see the Satan of this fate.

(1973)

Wild Escape

Wild escape, makes frugal plan,
And for a moment, still,
Regulating, with indifference,
And then, seem never there.

And contemplates for style,
Surveying where it, go,
Instants on insanity,
As in a wilds man eye.

A break, between the flow,
Perception at a touch,
And burst at such a magnitude,
That even, move, seems dull.

(1973)

A Smaller Thing

It was a smaller thing, than day,
And took a smallest need,
Momentary, least destruction,
Incidental death.

It seemed as safe, as lawn,
And by a glance, was out,
And by the glare of all the fixtures,
Hardly worth the loss.

My Tombless Grave

I smolder in my Tombless grave,
And feel no magic death,
And fingers pale at their insistence,
Clutching at their Skin.

To claw the walls which bind themselves
With nothing in, or out,
And worthless are the chains of Heaven,
That fall unlinking down.

I gird at these invisibles,
I cannot know to else,
To keep them powerful and mighty,
To wear the nothing out.

(1973)

The Last

I find no silence, but the last,
The rest, exterior,
Noises for the blood, or System,
Notes continuing.

The brain relaxes tracts of gauze,
Too distant, finally,
And thinks of ways she, used, to travel,
And contemplates herself.

She wraps faint bundles of the heart,
And seals them carefully,
Giving something for, remember,
Finishes her need.

The soul collects its wings, and opens,
Dusting them with air,
And while the currents, cease to nothing,
Dissolves, ethereal.

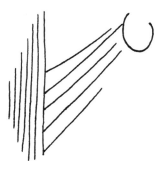

Behind the Landscape

We went to find the place she was,
Though I had never gone,
Felt it was, behind the landscape,
Or just, beyond the land.

We took a penny, for protection,
A rose for Quality,
And journeyed, where it seemed the safest,
Without ability.

We stopped and often asked the way,
Though listened predictably,
At some refusal, or some suggestion,
We'd thought of, Secretly.

The Momentary Fields

We are the momentary fields,
We are the passing light,
Memories of all our distance,
Pausing Bright.

We speak unheard of, Reveille,
Lifting in the Air,
Mornings held before the mornings,
Daylight everywhere.

And speak an instant, as we go,
Exploding Melody,
As if a Star had failed Existence,
And signed her Testament.

(1973)

Death is Least of Day

Death is least, of Day, Diers say,
Who ready out of Life,
Incidental to the Moment,
Preparations, sway.

We gage of, how much to be Lost,
Or how much Least, to gain,
Though the moment is forever,
Count it all the same.

As just another fate, at last,
Or just a passing, thing,
And find a trinket in the packing,
And reminisce, the day.

And plan as all the Locks are bound,
Of what there is to, do,
And underestimate removal,
Then drop, just out of sight.

(1973)

And Loss Remain

It is the loss of being, daily keep,
Like stones into me fit
Where there were places that ago
Had scented with elixers of fur and tail.

And were light, the more we joined,
Were bright, though we sought dark,
And solitude, were inhabited
As if in minions joined.

We moved a timeless step away,
We never parted for a day,
We slept as one, through boundaries run,
Though different, became the same,

A family not by name,
Though interior bonded, like flame,
Were burning ourselves to energy reclaimed
From our separate selves.

We were the thing that all desire,
To possess and then expire into one,
The evolution of love, to consume
And marvel at our diversity.

Though finite creatures holding divinity,
We did not pause to think
That flesh go out and temple fall,
And loss remain, though we had all.

(2006)

My Tomb

My tomb is loneliest, at day,
When I can feel the light,
And almost wish there was a window,
So I could look, about.

My room is granite, vast and square,
And has a vaulted door,
And just a bit of corridor,
And shelf, and lock, and I.

The centuries that must have gone,
Or moment, I can't tell,
Began it seemed when there was quiet,
And I was tiredest.

I had a candle, and a rose,
And heard the distant prayer,
Asking for a, safest journey,
As if I were going somewhere.

(1973)

The Lark

The news came softly, from the Lark,
And I, intent to hear,
Rose and listened with the silence,
For the cautious warbling.

The vowels were too dim, to spell,
He could not speak again,
Then ceased, unmoving, at the window,
And bowed a gentle head.

I thanked him for the sound most heard,
Then waited with the night,
To see if it was really something,
That day would never come to light.

(1973)

So Grown Accustomed

So grown accustomed, could I stand,
I'd search the hills for Tomb,
And lay soft down again, my fortress,
A special room.

And wait, or rot, whatever prospered
Such a simple place,
I'd magnify again for singularity,
And prate some silly vespers, heavenward.

It seems, because for life, have done
Sufficient, and my lands are sold,
And heirs just unremembering,
And fashion out of style for me,

And I have now no use, to move,
Except my lip, that mumbles in its shroud,
And heaven, not quite listening,
Being up so far.

(1974)

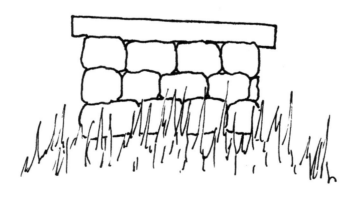

Who's Not Here Tonight

She'll look in caverns, with her light,
And strike the hungry den,
Knowing that, he must be there,
Lost behind a room.

She'll carry over mountains,
And wear the beaches out,
Turning every pebble back,
Asking, if they know.

Her eyes are dim, from shadows,
Taking up the light,
Asking with another sundown,
Who's not here tonight?

(1969)

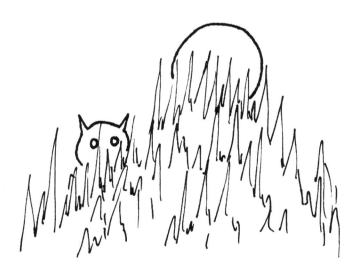

There is a Mourning

There is a mourning that stays live,
Processions, round the brain in dark,
It seems the tread would split a simple consciousness,
And crush within the maddened form.

As if the marchers had no grave,
Their sullen faces, moving on,
As if the death had yet to die,
Though given up its place in light.

And I remember, all the thing,
Its universe come down to me,
Like those, who cannot rest in death,
Their legacy of memory never having past.

And on the place, as easy to be there
As breath, the old trees bloomed afresh,
And on it reconstructing what we were,
The thousandth time again.

And on, no change except the feeling, of a loss,
Their movements, distant from my lingering
To speak, to reach the phantoms in their hideaway,
And hold them, in a gentleness.

Sown to Parch

This season, it seems
The spring without a seed to grow
Come gentle, when I must have slept
Some wakeless yesterday of night,

To now, in ever sunlight,
Where the thought of green
Condemn its thinkers to all evidence,
That they are sown to parch,

And crack the barren ground each step,
They linger at the soil,
Until a whiteness covers, in its freezing,
Clench a numb they will not feel.

(1975)

The Grave is Done

The grave is done,
The fields are rotted by,
And trees no longer standing by the hillside,
Are blackened to their stumps in soft decay.

Upon my moveless fate, to still,
The losses crack my yellowed bones
Inside the seeming flesh I carry, worthless,
To this spot, each moment that I think

To breathe another stifled breath.
For pain continual to thrive
At body's length, upon such agony,
I touch at intervals to know

That I can feel some instance
For respite, or movement that may change
The excommunication at my sight,
And blind, or distance me from knowing

That no trial is less than all eternity.
Except the never changing seems like change,
Sometimes at gasp, when flooding oxygen,
Like hope, gives seeming
Stimulation to the desperation.

(1975)

So Safe The Thought

So safe the thought of die,
No dungeon low enough to keep,
No pain too strong to last,
Too long.

Except the fear that we may die
Upon some crest, and happiest,
Loved at our side, combed and kept,
Just awakening at last in bliss.

Or just before the war is done,
Captain almost at the wall,
We fade, the hand about to touch
Our withered hand, a moment late.

(1975)

To Die

To die today, I think
To hear the funeral come,
With pennies for my hardened eyes,
And stone for ears.

And stiffness for my length of skin
And everything inside,
And sleep until eternity
Unhinged the molecules.

(1976)

Small Moments

At day, small moments pass by
To lives unneeding of their gain,
Unnecessary business, light unused,
Spanning just for others, in their need.

The house is full, the doors are done,
And to no window creep,
Survivors of a once day, hidden past time,
To where no other come.

Their choice is still, the lid come down,
And on it quiet thought,
Of minds preparing for another world,
To pause, and leave no clue.

`(1978)

The Gowns I Wear

I linger at the gowns I wear,
I brush a faded hem,
And stare straight into majesty
That come to take me in.

How slight she is, I thought a queen,
Or magistrate, or more,
Or pomp, or messages before she came,
Or jewels in her hair.

How plain this wedding dress for me,
I thought my own would be of gossamer,
And as I follow, simple to the silent hall,
Leave all else, and grasp these remnants
To be grand.

(1978)

There is a Moment

There is a Moment, set to Die,
A momentary place,
Incidental, Superficial,
Happening at last.

Though passed the spot, in greater Awe,
That It would feel so small,
And fainted as the world continued,
Cumbersome, along.

And oh, remember what, the thing,
To worry so, about,
Had passed unnoticed, but to Stiffen,
And blind ourself in doubt.

(1973)

Except to Death

I am dull except to death,
Who will not let me fail,
And secret me in his kind chambers,
And woo me there, and though I am not dead,
Keep me in his embrace to love.

For I am in love, and death with me,
And though my heart remain, it need not be,
And but to die, some useless act,
For where I shall be gone,
No movement of any, shall ever track.

(1973)

Like Single Agony

Like single agony, a silent death
Inside the form go out,
No notices from outer feeling,
No question to the heart.

No resurrection past the day,
The hours all akin,
Continue as they have always been,
And we are brought along.

Till suddenly, the moments come,
And take us to the spot,
The loss arrive at housetops,
And we are perishing.

The funeral bell exclaims its day,
The mourners spread a mile,
And suffer like the ages opened,
And time left everything.

(1978)

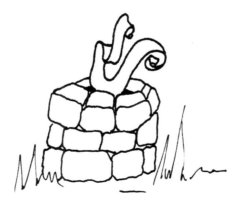

Start of Day

Death is start of day, say perennial.
We earn by just a season, and a fruit,
And coverlet of snow,
And like we had not lived at all,

Begin again the thing we do.
Though there are remnants in the houses,
Just a memory, or faded flower in some drawer,
That we had been.

And it is like an adding to the same,
That is not lost or gained,
But seem an all when we are dowered
In some petal grove.

But at some lives, a loss they could not fathom come,
Till calculations stop eternity,
And they do not desire to renew,
But having had the thing, reject the time again,
To be some hidden beauty that repeat,
As if it never had been gone.

(1979)

A Little Death

A little death went out today,
And all the spirit vapors came,
To mourn it with a silence
That comes from such an end.

No toll in dell, no senses for the thing,
We cannot print upon a stone
To register its decay,
Or place its memory as a trinket
In some hideaway of thought.

It is these passing moments that we hold so well,
The greatest loss is frugal at her birth
To time, and circumstance of all we are,
And fit completely, thoughtlessly in us.

It is the thing that we remember at the last.
Fortunes all upon the empty space could not provide
A filling in, and we are hopeless bound,
Unknowing, except the feel of chain.

(1979)

The Last Escape

The forest is aflame,
Its heat turn to wild creatures
Cramped at the edge, for no place to run,
At the last they faint
Into a melt of the horror thing
That come at their life, eyes skulling in,
Ears achoke to feel the noise that come
Thumping in their heads,
While they quiver to the loss
Of place to hide.

And the terror monster lift them to the sun,
At light to show all edges, and all,
And creature clap silent in his brain
To take the last escape.

(1979)

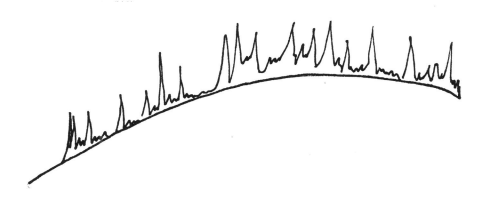

The Stilling Form

It was as same as any moment,
The clocks recording when the end came
Within, their steadiness, reflector
Of the stilling form.

The tick, the last register of when the finish
Turned firmward within the self,
Its eyes accustomed to a dark
No longer at the light.

And strange relief at last at being done,
As if a message come from life
To say that we are dead,
And form continue out of habit,

Toward some destiny of breath or fail,
While in the body we unhook
From senses, useless, having less the need
To search for findless things.

(1981)

There is a Sense

There is a sense, no notice of,
Come to the form, till death
Remove it from its place of chance,
And press it into stone.

No feeling of the pass of time,
As if continuous worlds linked,
And stretched the being out,
Into eternity of consciousness.

As if at safe, it stayed all whole,
No increment, or fading
Towards the spot called end,
It seem there could not be, but self.

A point of where the thoughts unite,
Some magic, special place,
Come through somehow to bear the destiny,
And judgment, of what senses find.

The Searing Act is Done

The searing act is done,
The death of him has come,
Old fury speak, needless pressing in,
It is the day beyond the loss.

When outward sorrows cease,
When silence come like golem raised,
To haunt us where the love had been
To take the place of then.

We lean towards north, to cold,
To isolation where here had been touch,
To less of everything,
To waiting, though not for a thing.

It is the grief plateau,
Not summit or depth, or raging agony,
Or flailing, helpless grasp
Onto the still body.

It is the having put away of scene,
Of what is left to do,
To settle on the flat, arid surface
Surrounded by oblivion.

(2008)

Zippy

With this death, departs the world
I held in balance in the universe,
Now hardened, in its separation from being whole,
And fractured, like a thing

Put into drawers that has no use,
At each moment, mindless in its moveless form.
Not to remember now, what I had been,
So sharp replaced the possibility of then,

That once day, when a younger self
Was a happy guiding for all happening,
Now crushed out of inner reason,
Like some judgment passed.

And there the sorrow sound in grief,
Opening new possibilities of depth
From aches it felt,
As if there were no boundary for loss.

There is a Stilling

There is a stilling at the place
We do not give a name,
As if some ancient clock had finished,
Long past its sires, whose world depleted

With their going out,
And laden with the touch they fondly
Placed, kept track of their demise
Since then, having been set
To regulate this habitat.

As if some great machinery went on,
And we, at dark, accustomed
To its place, linger against its cool foundation,
Some primal sound.

Until the sound go out,
Then, we slowly wander from the monument,
Its memory unable to contain us,
And we unable to repair its loss.

(1986)

A Death

There is a death no sense reveal,
No loss amid receptors at the brain,
Its network to perform continual,
As if machined by sensibility.

Yet ghostly senses parallel,
Which hungering for invisible stimulation,
Turn dull, unaided by a memory
Of when sustenance was carried
To this other self.

Though helpless to move,
Or change, or act upon,
This strange, elusive thing, unseen,
Like roots, gave nourishing stability.
Gave presence that spark perception
Of life's source.

Now carry on our neutered, mindless fate,
And dust a stair, and order,
And arrange our habitat,
As empty outward, as within.

(1982)

A Self

The thing we call a self,
Some sense brought being,
Crystaled, till its form go out,
And we are particle of ocean, or of else.

Somehow survivor to continuum,
Life's steady vehicle, as if imprinted in us,
Deeply to the circle we spin,
Round something, hold.

And am a lit beam, kindling
Into that furtherest habitat, fartherest edge,
No one imagined was existing,
Having been so far away.

The grope to it , to stretch,
The constellation face of us there, eyes of stars,
Beyond ordered matter, now conscious awakening,
Compose the ability to touch eternity.

The Loss

The loss begins like particles,
Till we are old,
As if some movement finally stopped,
Reverberating to the sound,
Till clock says still.
And ancients settle, by the hush,
Their crinkled hems now in some drawer,
And once agos reflected to a print, or page,
And all comes dark within.

Beyond Ability

Beyond ability, some remnant lie,
Unable to achieve its aching immortality
Into light, some invisible sun
We turn our faces to.

It warm the secret places,
No light can enter in to this higher self,
That is elusive throughout all life,
Come dreamlike in its desire to awake in its reality.

We moan alike the nights of creation,
To be born into the spot,
And ply our fingers to discover
Where the homestead is,

And then at last go out.
Who knows the destiny of consciousness,
Its only remembrance at shroud,
Reveal the similarity of search
Of generations who have been.

Life's Journey

4. Love

Yank and Pull Your Hair

If we could kiss it would be cute,
Then make you suck upon my boot,
To get to know your different ways,
And leave your brain all in a haze.

To put you in a bottle clear,
And then to learn to call you dear,
To mount you on a board would be no sin,
And then I'd stick you with a pin.

It would not be too hard to do,
To roll you in a pot of glue,
And stick some feathers on your head,
And tuck you firmly in my bed.

To drag you down the road some day,
Would be my favorite form of play,
And make you lift me on your back,
While you are standing on a tack.

I hope to see you down the lane,
Because you give me a great big pain,
You make me want to hold your hand,
While trying to bury you with sand.

It must be your great big laugh, I think,
That makes me want to push you in the drink.
To squeeze you till your lips turn blue,
Is just a portion of what I'd like to do, to you!

(2007)

Take Me To The Place

Take me to the place where you have been,
For I am tired now and cannot find it,
Where you have spread yourself out naked,
Not in the dark, not hidden,

Because shadows are shameful things,
And I can feel your light, and see my hand
Pressing your shoulder down upon me,
And holding you as if you were myself.

Same heat, same suppled flesh into me,
I remember when I broke through, like ice
Cracking, and I was suddenly submerged,
And the cold was warm.

And to think was turned off, like death,
Some altered state as natural as breath,
And I was gasping there,
Mouth juices splattering on my face from you.

And I could not tell the moment there,
Or where I was, so closely were you breathing
In me, that it was another consciousness
That stepped into us, that we were complete.

I do not know where that place is now.
I think it was from touching that we led ourselves.
It was a different movement
Than traveling, as if we chanced into a magic zone,

And I was full in you, and done,
And since have not desired again,
For nothing now is more valuable or real,
Since I became you, and all of life was felt.

(2002)

The Mountain Issue

The mountain issue grows still,
Here on his sometimes bed,
Older than the hills, and wise,
Come down here gently,

As the quiet is his air.
Beast of affection, I lean into him,
Held by calculations of a loss
That could never right me again.

We dare because we are close,
Here in this silent room,
Found and safe, somehow needing shore,
Needing to stretch ourselves

To see that we are still whole.
While the wreck remains out there,
Our fortunes tossed with it,
We are safe here, momentarily.

No tomorrows will come
To haul us back, somewhere,
For this embrace is endless,
And will be felt when there is seemingly
Nothing more to feel.

(2002)

Riker

I cherish what enlightens,
Small time things that led to solitude,
That have transcended family,
Have moved beyond society.

Have found station here, alone
With beast who brings wild scent,
Its earth tones calming,
Its eyes radioactive in sincerity.

It is my beast, what does remain
To me from all firmaments,
This more than precious form,
Substantial in stability,

Stark in dedication of its home,
We linger, this is momentarily bright,
This is temporarily alight,
This is unexplainedly delight!

(2006)

All My Senses

So perfect, all my senses fled,
As brave as worthiness,
To beg a longer vision past the solitude,
To where he touched, to touch again.

And lay my weathered form on his,
And balm me in the life,
From once where I knew so suddenly
The ravages of drought.

And how so dungeoned, when I thought to move,
As visible as feel, the chain
That pull me from the knowing,
Where I might have met him, light to light.

And now the dim, a clear accustomed to itself,
We grow more common to the shade,
As loneliness, a fragile name for numb,
Spread into how we could have loved.

(1976)

Dead Song

Why did you throw me away?
Your touch began to feel like a fist,
You looks were glass eye doll looks,
And then you stopped looking.

You wanted hurry up hard sex.
Just do it, faster and faster,
Looking out train window sex,
Fucking through glass sex.

I began not to be there sex,
I began to go to hell sex,
Leave me alone sex,
I'm dead sex.

Keep away from me, fever touch,
Because I am thrown away,
Don't you remember?
Used up tube, useless, thrown away.

Why do you get further away,
The closer you get?
Shut down systems, shields up
Kind of away.

And you don't want to hear about it.
Always in rooms, we spend our lives
In rooms staying together,
Away from each other.

(1999)

Departed Sweet

Departed sweet, upon myself
The looping memories entwine
In momentary things, a thought of breath,
In the still, a gentle touch, for me.

A passion so controlled in form,
Its perfectness a millionth time might be,
Just need enough to love, in holding,
Vision in material.

But just as difficult, the day intrude,
And spread its masses in,
And leave no room for seeming incidental,
And keep the samest sharp.

No magic here, the gowns are dust
We could have fled in to our happiness,
So to the darkness, at a nakedness,
Strive the waiting moments in.

And put our solitude in draws,
And care less for the dream again.
Its grandness higher than our foot could step,
And we still lower for its loss.

(1976)

When You Go

I'll not alter when you, go,
You'll be other where,
And what I find left to, breathe,
Will, satisfy, the air.

Birds fly in it,
Leaves, do,
They'll not mind a stony weight,
When I attempt to, aviate.

He Calls

He calls from little islands,
When I've gone away,
Burning through, fog, and night,
Like, dreams.

I thought I could, reach him, there,
For lonely nights to see,
Constant beam of guarding,
For ships, for him, and me.

(1968)

Why Should I Love You?

Why should I love you
If you are true,
And braid my hair, to wait,
Satisfied and punctual, content,

And buy a cat and chair,
With smiles on my fading lip,
Read to you romances daring,
When mine is guaranteed.

I should be free if you are not,
Tempt and win with lies,
And sleep with you and call for others,
Then see only you in their eyes.

If you are faithful, I am false,
Will worry you at last,
And settle down when I am weary,
Without a rocking chair, or shall,
And go to sleep.

(1972)

Finish to a Sigh

Had I to send, 'twould give to him
A packet of my care,
Ribboned with a fit of passion,
And stamped from everywhere.

To be true to anyone,
Until I cannot be,
Then wonder how I came to worship,
Unnecessarily.

Teach myself with rhymes and psalms,
And supplicate with woe,
Then finish to a sigh, and moving,
Ride me out of sight.

(1969)

The Loss

I fear no other than the loss,
I would no longer feel,
Caring just again for others,
In some expected place, and way.

Carefully invite in reason,
Express more cautiously,
Value placed upon its value,
Packaging for use.

I would no longer speculate,
Upon the chance of bliss,
Its steeply polished, soaring heights,
A view somehow, be missed.

The lingering of first sought love,
The place where it had been,
Becomes a distant memory,
Of why, and how, and when.

(1973)

This Loss

This loss is better, because it goes,
And we can feel the space,
And lease the room where used to fill us,
And now a waiting thing, to sell,

That seems the same, the walls still hold,
But to remembering,
Call boundary from its chest, and closet,
Dark clothes we never thought to wear.

(1973)

To My Spirit

He is dull, and I am helpful
To keep him fair,
And give, oh the give is generosity,
With no investment, there.

And to my spirit, silence, with a kiss,
For where the pain is deep,
Little possibility come, and with us weep
For none to care.

But of these things, remind ourselves,
We are waiting all together,
And only need the satisfaction of Grace,
To write us and melt the world.

(1973)

Angel

Angel, I have kissed your webbed feet,
And exposed myself to mockery and cold,
And traveled for you,
And run the chance of being untrue.

But for what benefit, this trial?
You have given me everything in return,
Dowaged me with palaces and love,
And only see me when I want.

But when I do, you always ask
Such simple things I would do for anyone.
You have legions for the difficult,
And God, the impossible.

You have made me forget where I have come from.
My calloused hands are smooth,
And shoulders sensitive in woven silk,
And my heart so silent, since we met.

(1974)

What Haunted Flower

What haunted flower this,
To bring its life on stem above a parching tract,
And open in still born air its ether scent,
Never having been explained
That paradise was once ago.

And cheek that to its petal might have pressed,
Now dust for elements to hoard away,
And we are different,
Than when it should have come.

Still joyous then, and life to life, would touch,
And circlet round, our diadems would place
On every head, and growing magnitude
Of glory lush our home with satisfaction,
That there was so much to do.

And we had all the time,
We, pale survivors, creeping at the darkness,
Chance upon this too late flower,
Weeping in its beauty, that we are too dry to touch.

(1974)

So Close To Fortune

So close to fortune, would I breathe,
Into the holy hall arrive
In majesty, with weddings for my mind,
And funeral, ago.

And busy mystics in their stations,
Printing diadems, my size,
And diamond shoes, and carpets spun of web,
And ether gowns of perfect quality.

And there who all I love the best,
Each moment of him, mine,
And deep into his sinews listen
For his blood for mine.

And circle him in golden rains,
And make him in myself,
And quiet in our passions linger,
To stretch the harmony.

And kiss him full of balm and light,
And turn our beings round
To make us wonderful in unity,
And marvelous delight.

But hold my breath upon the thought,
Some secret to my mind,
That in a limitation, in my loneliness,
The wanting all too sweet to pass.

(1975)

As Close To Love

I am as close to love, as touch,
And out my hand extend
Its tender points, reached dangerous
To that mysterious area, in shroud.

What is within that grasp, the hold,
I cannot tell as yet,
But change within already marks me,
Caught, to risk the arm,

And fling myself fresh brought to this place,
Towards my goal and purpose be,
Now daring, daring to expose too quickly,
This barely pink experience, on eternity.

(1975)

Would I Love

Would I love, I'd turn my room
Into a crack of day,
And smooth my apron at the prospect,
And think to tie my hair,

And rearrange the chairs for two,
And put a flower out,
And polish in my eyes, the longing
Of the specialness.

I'd bring an oval ring to wear,
And lace my better shoes in hope,
And look along the door,
As if its next belonging through,
Came an everything.

But to the thought of move, from here,
So dangerous at stiff immobility,
That I may lose the strength to loosen,
If he ever came.

(1975)

Touch Defenceless

The distance, not in space, is measured
Between a reach, to touch,
Though engines strong could never move the self,
Desire fail its lunge to grasp.

Effort hardly put could master it,
The moment easily would gain,
And some achieve it,
Some possess, carelessly enfolding,

Their shrill meaty beings entwining,
And unaffected, move on.
But to touch defenseless,
The primal inner beast alert,

And checks the move.
This hidden thing that cannot heal
Once slapped away, once cold eyed
Pushed away, once jerked from its fingers,

Cannot extend its fragile arm,
Though there are mountains' strength behind it,
It looks out, only, silent seeking,
Despite the need to hold.

(2017)

An Achy Heart

There is an achy heart I know,
Who longs for touch, who does not grow,
Mired in a dollop of some caramel,
His sticky fingers, out of his hell

Reach me, and smear my torso
As I ascend dragon beasts, and ride
Horned, scaled, hided lizard things
To some glory behind the shelf.

It is enough to do, my work,
Without this saddened thing looking to me,
Like lost puppies look to tender eyes,
Like hungered, need-bound, creatures look.

And makes a sound, a whimpering
While he is speaking, makes a cry
With his body heat, to me
For some comfort, comes to try.

And I notice him, though he is shy.
Missed fortune's mark, doesn't know why,
Slipped up, lonely, gone dry,
This boy with hunted eyes comes by.

(2007)

Silence into Sensation

The urge to be soft,
To be taken, done to,
Extricated from silence into sensation,
Brought forth like clay into fire,

Has the cost of emotion,
Handed over eagerly to some face
Who writes your name in a dark book,
And presses your finger against it,

Smeared in bodily fluid, to seal you,
To remove your ability to not feel,
The beast rides over you, heavy,
What heat bodies have!

What ability of stimulation,
That had been under clothing
And guarded by fists and eyes and mouths,
That sought you like heat missles

When you looked at shapes, and bulges,
Now on you! Sacred things
Now out of their chaucible, now on you,
Like acid must be like on you,

Pressing into your past the last holdout
Of physical resistance, touching momentarily,
How cold the solitariness becomes,
After. And how long the sting

Of separation lasts, the invisible scars ache,
The chafe of hard stiffening, not cock hard,
Not anticipation hard, tough hardening
To resist the longing that was desire formed.

(2006)

There is an Anger

There is an anger that I love to feel,
The searing scratching of poison ivy rash
Down to the blood, the digging of a thorn
To its piercing release in outrage
That the self be so afflicted

By something it has touched, some souvenir
Of something it reached for, like
It reached for you. Some putrifaction
On my fingertips from touching you.

What joy to recoil, such peace
To draw back from the flame of you,
Such rage to have experienced
So many almost unfelt stinging lies,

Like nettle bushes on my unsuspecting nakedness,
That grew into a torrent of pain
Because I was exposed to you,
Was stripped bare with you.

Vulnerable, unexpecting self flayed open
To expose my fire engine red interior,
That burned from microvenom droplets,
Spewed at your string tight lips

Upon my self,
To see if I would endure without expression,
Your slycat razor talons, tickling me,
While your slow smile pulled your face into a sneer.

(2007)

In Instants Flashed

What had been hope, becomes a memory
As we pass the place, or scene,
That brings to mind the longing
That had been there, now past.

How we had ever come to hope,
As if some magic sparked,
And we were drawn to luminescence
That pierced the dusk a moment,

And went out. But our eyes had seen
The pleasure of desire, though distantly,
Not close enough to touch or grasp,
Not large enough to encompass us.

Not steady for a constant view of it,
The thing in instants flashed
Into us, and yet remained inside
So long, its passing took a part of us.

(2007)

The Hope of Touch

It is the hope of touch we seek,
Though for some, not invested of a hand,
Or face to move in passion zone,
But message send, while he remain apart.

And will not know the magnitude of reach,
It is as alien, yet common to the herd
To be so courted for a hold
Of recognizability, that we belong.

From cave or peak, some room display
The temple, where this hermit stand,
Who looks within and sees without,
Who motions in the silence and the noise is moved

To seek this homespun enlightenment.
Though do not grasp the place, or form,
Do not express it knowingly,
The creature desire to be held by touch,

His loins to wrap it round and push
Into it, to express his need
Where words cannot embrace,
Where logic slip, his male scent flow.

(2006)

The Best Achievement is Touch

The best achievement is touch,
Though to maintain instants
Great engines burn, gears twist
In hidden maintenance of magnitude.

The seeming gentle reach destroys
Foundations of girder,
Ledge cracked with weight,
The soughing of breath at lips

Trembles unseen support
When flesh touch. The greatest strain
Is unknown, shattered bedrock,
Though unexpected in seeming ease,

Practical motion of fingers reaching,
Will not betray its cost,
Like adrenaline can mask pain
And push great strength, unknowingly.

Momentarily achieve some summit,
In instants gaze over having leapt,
Extend fiercely, that, the great ability,
When that connection joins as one.

(2006)

Aroma'd at the Eyes

What is passion alarm this ancient man,
Who passed the site some century
When firm blood looked out haltingly,
And smelled the buck scent moving round.

Here, now, though the scent remain,
The man's desire holding still,
The age of reason fail,
Compatibility depart.

The lined face is not what inner fires
Feel, it feels bloated young, fully flesh'd,
Delusionally freshly sprung,
That even when so, back ago, did not so clearly state

This wrenching, pulsing, blooded thing
That man flesh stimulate,
Till all is engulfed by it, all consumed,
Lingering there, aroma'd at the eyes.

How to express it,
To linger at or in it,
Its illusionary mountain form,
Gigantic as the stifled urge to touch.

(2006)

Where Memory Shifts

Now stilled, tight passion reigned,
But not the wanting, old drug,
Whose face has altered like soft wax,
Where memory shifts.

And this next man, seeming desperate
In his familiarty, is part me,
The magnitude of attraction
To the degree of my desire expressed.

But there is something in the touch,
A flavor unknown, yet wanted,
A smell and sound primal felt,
So that the hand goes deep in me.

But it finally is the solitude that lasts,
The man flees, unconsumated,
Unexposed, his reserve like sheets between us,
Leaves me virginal, and silent, and still.

(2005)

Selfish Habits

Foreign habits contain him,
Which consume him in silence
From me, though I am master
Of silence, cannot reach his touch.

Some old routine attends him,
Like some moneyed courtisan
That in a rare gift dispenses
Her wealth to contain him.

But I am not bright enough
To attract him from distances,
Like beacons turning, not
Attractive like his familiar circumstance,

To include me, who would engulf
His air. Who would possess him,
Like tumors growing in him,
Who would enter, and explode what makes him.

(2005)

What is Unused

To place what is unused away,
What cannot be had alone,
Takes a courage unnoticed by many,
Takes a silence mostly overlooked.

As if there were no dwelling place within,
The sinewed flesh continue in its contstancy
And what is only visible maintain,
And what is momentary, control.

But there are rooms behind the face,
Not calculated, or in particle perceive,
The feeding of it chanced, like scavengers,
Though its potential crush or fill a life.

(2005)

Who Ply the Mudded Swamp

Who ply the mudded swamp persist
On purpose, not summer pause
Into bounty, not careless silence
On landscape, familiar in its touch.

It is the uncontrollable thing,
The landscape lush in unknown,
Fetid in decay fed from growth,
Silent, yet undertowed with passion.

It is the place we dare to go.
It is the openess of reach
Beyond our room, its door is wet
In moss, its threshold dank.

Yet I prepare to go, to tread it,
To wallow in thick mud,
To seek in my purpose that dark hand
To on me touch, and pull me in itself.

(2005)

What Draws the Self

What draws the self to other selves
Lies open in a helpless naiveté
For purity of touch. It is the depth
Of long need, to station childlike clear.

To reach yieldingly, the deep press
Into internal workings reach
As dangerously as senses stilled,
As we push outward, mindlessly,

Hopelessly, the chasm undefinable
In its width, and we are blind.
To try the space without illusion
Sparks the possibility of chance,

Though slim, without control of what we seek.
The movement there beyond our hand
Exerts itself, its own agenda changing,
Its needs resolving, loses sight of me.

(2005)

Silence at a Distance

Silence at such a distance, is this home.
To look out at boundaries lined across land,
The quieting for want of substance to be loud,
In this external view of space.

This is not the place of bold activity.
Secret gestures, small dance-like movement
Rounded in some silk to imagined courtiers,
To step in gown, evoke another, younger self to be.

This is where the grey being pause,
And his shapeless, dim being rise,
Though cotillions are done,
And men are vapors like sick rooms lingering

In their scent, though the illness passed.
They are what the noise was for.
They are what the touch could sound in me,
And voice in moan, not calculated,

Not predicted, the language they would speak.
Their tongues like man lips parting
To reveal a celebration, not required to dress,
And that moment of departure, mouthed speechless goodbye.

(2005)

We are Less Whole

We are less whole who have experienced,
Who have ventured out
Beyond our reaches of safe, of nest,
That are silted back into some hidden place.

What draws us is the light.
Seeming green, warm, vibrant, cascading
Of fracturing beams in color, allure us,
It is the thing of discovery.

It is a time to go.
Our loins ache to be consumated, we go,
From the darkness out, into what
Appears beyond the garden.

And we would turn, momentarily,
To return to what we knew,
But is no more. The den is lost,
The home, the price, taken for our destiny.

(2003)

This Structur'd Thing

Timber of fur, foundation of bone,
Glossed cinnamon eyes, racks of ear,
Sphinx shank'd, mottled 'n dottled,
Old black and white before technicolor'd dog,

This structur'd thing, this firmament,
Whose observation deck'd view ignite
Into me like spears, like recognition
That symbiotically we wed.

Join in paths ahead, the forest tread,
Join'd in bed at senations which allow
Our bonding stead,
This one and I have led familiarity.

A chanc't meeting, hearts so beating,
Passion'd seething till we bond'd,
And from drug'd hazing, faded,
Have learn't sobriety a bearable society.

(2006)

Hapless Wanderer

To touch is observation cursed,
The temple fouled, or worse,
The agony of self confronted,
With the burden of another skin.

Which to get to know is jagged,
Like rocks, picking through assumptions
To discredit or discard, or worse,
To remain.

It is the agony of sex, to linger,
When the possibility suppose itself
To stimulate on another, which is worse
Than on yourself.

The trial of another, some weakened victim
Who weary falls on you and calls it home,
Misguided brother, no more to roam,
Hapless wanderer, together, alone.

(2006)

I Almost Loved

I almost loved, so close the burn,
That could I gage the heat,
Would send its fire to my frozen face,
Feeling that it was,

Like silver piled in beams to spend,
Like magic for a step,
Like crystal in each inch of being,
Tapestries of yes.

I almost thought my room enough,
Connected when it came
To palaces of mile and fortress,
And a space for me.

And as I was about to give,
The news that I must wear a crown,
Reduced me hopelessly in tremble,
In the fear of grand.

(1975)

Some Other Land

Passioned without skill, our will
To gird upon a thigh of thought,
Some other land, or speculation,
Better suited for contemplation.

Place of pain we worship now,
Our bloodied fruit soon dry
Upon the tribulation altar,
Given to the gods of sky.

(1975)

Stopless Changed

Loss is painless as it goes,
The numbed tooth ripped from feeling,
Leaves no scream as testament,
Of its last agony at life.

The moment we are there, depart the plan
Of our survival, world at still,
Unleashed at last to burden, or remove
Our fainted state of holocaust.

Doomed the chore of thought,
Where senses clear removed, tap smooth no more,
One last position at that moment,
Then we are stopless changed.

(1975)

My Season of Despair

The garden laced with rot is where I lie,
Upon the frost slashed beds of blackened green,
Where flowers might have been one day,
For others to envision,
Who were endowed more generous,
And fit to be allowed to rise, when sun
Screened mistily by the heavy blooms of incense,
Laden full of color
On their fattened stems of pastel touch,
Enjoining with the brick firm paths,
To where some lady sat in tightened satin
Round her joyous waist of mansought bliss.

(Continued)

I, left shivering,
Am bramble tossed beside the bench
Her gowns there gently settled on.
I bruise beside the path his ice black boots
Have leather touched, in firm, still motion,
Rising to the muscles
That extended to her outstretched hand,
In pressing his perfected lips
Upon the dust ground powder that she wore.

I lie still, here in the damp,
This moisture pressed upon me
Might have beautied flowers once ago,
Though I can only think to wonder
Why some other, wrapt in holding arms,
Casting all upon the senseless beauty
That I would have forfeited myself to be,
To have him touch me.
Ever soft, yet forceful,
From insistent mouth, and eyes,
Melting my eyes to his,
I would have given everything
To feel that glance, so reckless given,
To be that object of desire,
But to this bed, where I enjoy
The fading light, and solitude,
That seems to balm me as the night advance,
I lie colder than the hardened ground,
So seem to warm here, in my season of despair.

(1975)

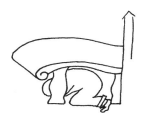

Some Silence

Some silence in the night, entwine
Inside me, like a sleeping thought,
No special message, to my untouched ears,
No mission, for the fingers by themselves.

Just alone, the moments spread,
As if eternity came down,
And formed me in its waiting holiness,
And bound my every in.

Asleep almost, the pulse like any other,
Seem some careful regularity
To hold me, like some arms around my solitariness,
That dulls the thought of you.

(1975)

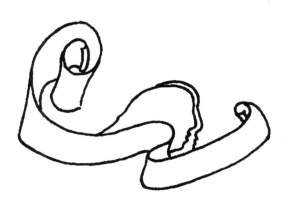

This Dream

Beauty, where the heavens meet,
Eternity to eternity, you, from long have come,
And candled in my gown,
I wait upon the greatest door,
To fling it for the finder, when he, on it, touch.

And know I am beyond, and to me reach,
Yet gods at worlds, have easier controlled
Their universes, than I could have moved the door,
And to you come.

For waiting all this life, for just one purpose,
In my sacrifice to gain the push, and
Void on void all balanced rush
To you, as if I could, through merit, or excuse.

Some moment, I hear the breath, and nearer be,
Locked here in my simple dungeon,
Fainting at each minute, just with Hope,
That each is worth its passing, and someday
Prove that just a dream was true.

(1975)

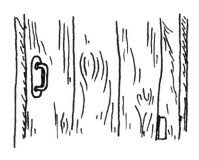

I Link Into Myself

As perfect as my mind could stretch,
I link into myself
The vision of a special being,
Come silent as a secret mystery.

And sit upon my ancient chair,
And to the day I wait all through,
And plait and bind,
And listen as the rays go down.

And sit into the garden, stilling,
As quiet as a hush,
And to the well laid flowers
Scenting in their pattern rows,
Station on my bench.

And in an inch of mind extreme,
The being come,
As wonderful as all imagining,
And movement unrequired there, to touch.

So sit, and when the moon display,
I think him into sight,
And far behind my lips, are kissing
In unknown delight.

(1975)

In Moonbeam Circle

We walked in moonbeam circle,
Round the black soft place, now hallowed
In its dark, no more a field.

Its grasses slick with holy water,
That we dared upon,
Its boundary of tree, now citadels
Of magic touch, and you held all my hand in warm,
And softly we approached.

And slowly we were all transform,
Our lips so tingled that each breath was taste,
And we clung tightly to our forms,
Now kneeling at each other, waist in arm,
And pulled upon the ground some pagan lust.

And moan alike the winds, baptismal sound,
And time was out of date, and all I can remember
Is the cold, each time at memory
You come to haunt me, in my heated room.

(1975)

The Crew is in the Wood

The crew is in the wood,
Simplified and good,
Gaining with the act pertaining,
Being at their habitat.

Mission without ill, being still,
And doing fortitude,
Extended curiosity, therein,
Contemplate within.

Pacts of play necessity,
Conditioned unity,
Dancing with a forest, prancing,
At the wind, facing in.

Dusty plain folk, daubed in dew,
Rustling the air,
Everything pertains together,
Dotes this crowded few.

(1972)

Animal in Wood

At long the vision come, the memory upturned,
Now formed of wet hard bodies
Where we, wild, uncivilized,
Are animal in wood.

Where we trample flowers in our lust,
And sing a field-song scream at passion,
Where we linger at the break of forest,
To listen for the wind,

And smell our kind, in mingled, on the damp
Of special place, where we belong.
Our touch molding everything to animal,
Clean upon the streams, dip silent ripple.

(1975)

The Surface Rainbow Brew

The mists today that circle
Round in particle, and bit of longing,
Move to whenever we were young enough,
To stand as tall as weed and big as air.

When we were fresh experience,
The world on golden hinges moved,
To every season, sparkled in its new vitality,
And we were there to greet it, greeting us.

The timeless speed, that reached to us,
Bitter in its seed was there,
At happiness, dredged in our crystal bowl,
And we drank deep the surface rainbow brew.

(1975)

In Dust

Out of love, I spread my wispy memories
Against the cold and light,
Of when I was protected, held in gentle arms,
In silent comfort at some still of dusk,

And kissed until I melted in the soft.
Each urgent and encompassed dream came true,
And I was filled with all his breathing
In my body, and each sigh combined us to ourselves.

And everything was holy where we were,
As if we were encastled into gold,
Embalmed in such a glaze that sun delighted
To display herself, and every thought was majesty.

And like a veil, the world was sweet,
And touched us with its silk,
And like a vapor to my mind, remembering, somehow
It fled, and turned me all but pain, in dust.

(1976)

Amid the Still

We stopped amid the still one dusk,
Unmoving as it took us in,
And ancient were the fields upon us,
Spreading at themselves,

Stimulation at a mooring as the damp began.
And arm in hand I led him through,
The moon was out of light,
And paused, the edge of forest still as wall,

And sound was silent as the feeling,
As I touched him round.
And spread his lips upon my face,
And felt him weight upon me at the ground.

And pound my heartbeat through his fingers,
Grasped unthinking, bound.
Until my soul fled into his,
As if the mansion burned,

And smelted homeless at his doorstep,
Turned, helpless, at his chest
An offering for gods,
Though deity had never chosen to accept.

(1976)

An Emptiness

I link an emptiness
Around me as a hope that I still feel,
And I am ready to begin again
Some lesser happiness.

The high shoes that we once could try
Are bigger than a dream we dare,
The palaces that they find comfortable
Are foreign to our poverty.

I could not try the step in rag,
My apron where their gowns are spread,
Protect somehow too little near a satin habitat,
Where jewels ignite the sun.

And only in the dark, I try
My fingers on a dusty prayer
I seem to think of, from some memory,
That hold me like a chill.

(1976)

Into the Nothingness

How deep into the nothingness
We ship our bodies down,
Dismal in the want for satisfaction,
Hopeless drowned.

Helpless in our search for touch,
The ruin come, and come,
Till we are molded like the monster,
And take to breathing him.

(1976)

It Must be Day

It must be day, the walls seem bright,
And on my floor I can imagine
That the grass is warm,
And there are trees, circled round the little room.

There is a brook with moss, and eider ferns,
So fresh are everywhere,
And I am lying in the softness of the land,
And sun is always saying noon.

And there beside me, not a dream,
Someone will rest my head upon their chest,
To hear their life so beating in the still,
And I will comfort on the touch.

So loved, and beautiful, and safe,
I will be perfect there
Upon that vision of eternity,
That takes a moment to be true.

(1976)

The Silent Balm

To feel the sorrow of the heart,
Is like a wounded thing
Who gazes to the air for comfort,
And finds the silent balm.

The heart for desperation hide
Its quiet in the mind,
Almost forgets the agony,
And thinks of other things.

Of how the universes bind,
Or why the ocean is,
And leave the little being spaces
To lie and feel a scar.

(1976)

To Love

To love is just as dangerous
As earth turned into teeth,
And passion spiking like a fever
To make delirious.

And dangerous as every pain
Could crowd into ourselves,
And stick a needle where the feeling
Grows into itself.

And sureless as a morning breath
Turned hopeless at the end of day,
And useless as a light to graveyards,
Or flowers people throw.

Or people and their image held
Like mirrors on a venom's tooth,
Like cancer fatefully enclosing,
Regardless of our will.

(1976)

Just Yesterday

I could have loved, just yesterday.
I had a satin gown put on,
And made my hair in braided circles,
And went about the town.

I had a ring of golden plate,
And shoes of antique pearl,
And rode to places in a carriage,
And it was summer, then.

But now, it seems a century
Went out of date, somehow,
And autumns fled me on a winter,
Hidden, at my room.

And as I sit amid the cold,
My fingers round a careful shall,
I wonder if the damp would enter me as deep
If I had more than cottons to put on.

(1976)

Safe

To dreaming passion that would he wake,
The earth her hinges bend,
To wait command from so alive the forces in him,
Beside me, lay asleep.

To love him, no, that age ago,
Too long without me would never recognize
Us here, though we are gentle in the night,
And safe the evening through.

(1976)

I'll Wait

If I were, pearl,
Upon your head,
I'd sit in jubilee,
Bowing now to pleasant guests,
And then to, royalty.

I'd dance with finest princess,
And touch her silken hair,
Polished with my own delight,
So stately, an affair.

When balls were done,
And guests away,
I'd sink on forehead, soft,
When princes and their lady, stay,
I'll wait.

The Palaces

Ruined are the palaces I knew,
Each king as dead as touch
Still lingering at memory,
Each castle fallen through to sky.

And so, I, willing in my life,
To polish every shattered kingdom stone,
Or bind the barren trees in soft,
And count them into safe,

Now wander in a blur of need,
On pavement, on a ruin land,
And choke as if the sky was thickened
To weight me into dust.

(1976)

So Late We Loved

So late we loved, the tired world just paused
Before us, lingering, and faded with the twilight,
Going out of date, and then was still,
And left us all in darkness at ourselves

To touch, and wonder where we felt,
Each moment unconnected in itself to join,
Since we were blind,
And could depend on only hand for sustenance.

And held each other softly through the blacking span,
Into our kisses lulled our bodies close,
And wakened in a dawning to alone,
Each, stranger, quickly running into day.

(1976)

The Sleeping Hour

It is the sleeping hour this year,
And if untired, we must wait
The season through, somehow surviving
With a memory of hope, or faded souvenir

Of once ago, when we felt young,
When we felt anything, so long
It seems in fading to this spot,
We should have turned to dust, some century.

What millionth mile is this, alone,
We seem to crawl amid the gutters
With some silent burden on our face,
And every thought is loneliness.

And every dream is vague of that someone
That will save us from ourselves,
And lift us, wrapped, protected in his arms,
And kiss away the sorrows that we keep.

(1976)

Some Moment Comes

This life, some moment come like bliss,
Its sight, as glories, as an omen,
Its feel so long, the moments linger,
As if they could extend

Their telling of forgotten things,
Some temple dropped a million centuries ago
And we could listen to, like fire,
And then become the flame.

Its presence calling, not to sense,
As if our bodies failed,
And we could hear in vapors,
And see in stone, and think in air.

And for one life, its coming, qualify
The birth, and leave a fragment
Not expressed by man, and key
To when the man is done.

(1977)

Foundations in the Soul

Further in my search for unity,
I dredge foundations in the soul
Of earth society, for memory,
Or future, of the possibility

Of golden temples, opened in,
Where moon sit in her holiness
To bathe on priestesses,
And bind a weighty power there.

In courtyards for our pagan rite,
Where I shall spread myself
Upon the colored silk,
And dedicate myself anew.

Let the passion then begin!
Rear its hidden head in silver-gold,
To light, and find us worshipping,
And worthy of its sacrament.

And lighter than we were before,
Our magic spread us
Like a single flag upon eternity,
And lick us with a special air.

(1977)

My Palaces

My palaces of day are done,
The world is out of sight,
And memory enwrapt in what it used to know,
And time, now quantity.

And what I might have offered some,
A miracle, or touch,
As antique as a duchess in a crown,
Within a citadel.

Royalty is out of date,
As foreign as a wish come true,
And so the passion, pack it into little drawers
To simplify escape.

(1977)

For the Passions

For all the passions of life,
That are so out of sight,
The urge remain, that to them all,
I still feel.

I still desire, now in this empty place,
That used to thrive with laden trees,
And each season one of fleshy harvest,
That the inhabitants fed upon.

I am of them who are in dust,
Whose ancient bones some cave contain,
And on them lust for hope
That I could touch again this life,
That hasn't been since centuries.

I'd Have Come

I'd have come, just one more, day,
When the trains, weren't too crowded.
I'd have had a, bonnet, on,
And leather shoes,
My newest velvet, gown.

Though easier than thought, to go,
To move, a sudden push,
I'd stand amid the doorway, then,
With light, upon me there.

Though easiest to do, the thing,
To make the motion to,
To go, a moment done, and then,
I would be there with you.

But an inability I did not know,
A stiffening within,
A holding to the quiet dimness,
I cannot turn without.

Better Lies

Had I spun better lies, to you,
I would have most believed,
Then suddenly to prove my honor,
Have broken all the ties.

And so declaring love at last,
You would have begged me near,
And supplicated with pretension,
And I, believing, give.

This Grace

This grace is not like other things,
It has no special name,
And seems to live on air and moments,
And bides where it is happiest.

No sorrow there, no thought of loss,
To it we must enjoin
By being only what it pleases,
And where it cares to go.

No thought cajoles, no bribe of gain,
No hope of fortune bless,
But all its worth to have upon us,
Like hunger to appreciate the feast.

(1978)

Another Place Than This

There is another place than this,
To be each moment. A silence
Lessens the grasp of station,
And the urge of possibility extend

Itself into a magic place. The room
Change now, its marble walls
Extend like palaces, and you are king
Of every one, and just as if

Some waiting ended, anticipation towards
The entertainment that becomes
A ritual of men, surrounding
Like a beat.

To enter in, where no balm
Could soothe the heat,
Comes loudest, near the consummation
Of touch.

(1981)

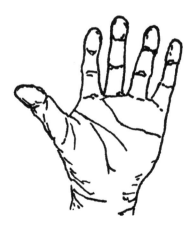

The Night of Dawn

That we must rise,
And think of something to be said,
It is the dawn, which must be fed,
A language not of kisses,
None of touch.

And we must rise, now soldierly,
Who stride a moment's pace apart,
But do not move, as we would like,
In the space of all still darkness
Where we would wish to lie.

Warm, and close, and silent,
As a paradise must be,
No harm could enter there,
For this was stuff that gods must give,

When they are kindly dispositioned
To be generous, and retract the claw,
As feline mothers do upon their young,
For even fleshly eaters
Can be merciful to what they spawn.

(1998)

Without Us

I've no will to love you, more,
Than I've loved, less,
No desire to reinvest.
Gone the spring, budded sweet,
Summers come, its folded wings
Bloom without us, there.

(1968)

There is a Pain

There is a pain that is not felt
Of nerves. It is outside the medic care,
Nor numbed at drug, nor colored
From pleasure or experience.

It is administered willfully, some old demon
Rising firm, like demon phallus, cold
Into the form it desires to penetrate,
Because we are soft and it is hard.

We are passion to it, a source alluring,
And it strikes, the venom poison,
Fast, toxic libation to the dammed,
Ingested into blood and being,

Consumation endlessly.
And its victim, wonder, where,
Before the damage come, what it was
To be before the fall.

(2003)

Though We Are Left

Though we are left behind, we are not stopped
By time, though we remain
Stationed to look out as if it were still
Youth, as if the passing
Was only other things, and we remained intact,

Not changed. It is desire that does not change.
We long to climb that heaving chest,
A cargo of jeweled treasures to adorn,
Though we are all the less

When we lay diamonds to our wrinkled neck.
For it is to be wanted
Where the treasure lay, that can alter
And youthen, and freshen, and free.

(2003)

Uncertain Times

Here, what seeks casually, appearing
At uncertain times for unfamiliar reasons,
And shares intensity, and leaves
Like dusk fogging out the light,

Lingers here like stiff shadows of dark.
He remains here, some head beat
Just the melody repeating further off now,
Keeps attending me.

Though what is the real man,
Has dispersed. Hardly recognizable, not familiar,
Like common things, his glass sharp edges
Prick me silently, no sound

But sounds that register in touch
To the senses, as if scent had tactile properties,
As if exposure of skin to skin had language,
And I grope to remember those words.

(2005)

That We Desire

It is not love that we desire
Who finish, finally, a life.
No moon-eyed gawking to ease us
Past breath. We are too old for that.

Who have lived when we would have kneeled
In fire for such a sweet embrace,
Are uncaring who could have been here
To send us off.

Late we grew to this freedom,
Blooming in the cold,
Of nature turned unnatural,
In peace where there is only barrenness.

Come, ghostly man, your vapors are my form
Where once was flesh.
Hurting blood that ached for touch,
Is gone out.

And I am no more the thing I knew,
Whose decrease of innocence
Enlarged this last spot where I retain a consciousness,
And become what I had been before I was.

(2002)

Male Musk

I sing the song that is not love.
Not that which you would sing to me,
Were you my man love under me
Not that which you would sing,

As I entered you in consumation,
Spreading you, until into you, out of control
I lose myself,
And grasp unknowingly,

As I feel the entering.
You are my male fuck whole man
Being, you are my heat,
Into my cock rages what you are.

I madly press until I cannot hold you more,
You are my madness come,
My ache to arch my back in you,
I come, I come my man male, come.

Though this is not an act of love,
It is not that which hearts shall hold,
Not this, which is ache to be felt,
I grasp into your ass, my fingers

Pressing on your ass, my passion
To be mated in you, you cannot
Stop this raging male musk,
Pounding into what is us, and us.

(1998)

As If There Were Tides

The passion recedes as if there were tides
Pulling from internal juices at some moon,
To still the cause of what had been so powerful
That sobriety snap as ground upon a fall.

And there is cause to breathe unsteadily.
The newfound footing shallow in its depth,
The careful turn of limbs uncertain
Where such appetite had gone without a feast.

Without a satiation in the groin,
The beast stir, blindly, tied into its flesh,
Remembers plains where it fed freely,
Feels yet the touch of quaking victim,

Its warm strike of taste as teeth rend it,
Its submission to claw containing it,
That was love. That wholeness in consuming,
That pain of entry, blood into blood

Was what maleness became in its full state.
Doubled upon male, its scent unbearable,
Unleashing fire burns that are like nectar fluid,
Cooling as they char, slashing as they heal.

That was comfort, home, a place.
This uncertain inability is blindness to need.
This loss of willingness is charnel,
Anger, what is more powerful than lust, remain alone.

(2005)

Black and White

This is the other side of life,
The side passed over what, in self
Was wholeness, like shattering,
The fragments, added, still contain the form,

Though altered, parting, what the memory
Of them as one grow brittle
Where it was fluid joy,
Transmute to desperate need.

I do not court the why of it,
Its distant form too far to grasp,
Its lure powerless to return me
To before, to the touch,

To the scent of it, to warm,
Contentment, to the breadth of it
Which was as much a part of me
As me.

Where I had extended into fur,
Had reached myself to fang and tail,
To cinnamon eyes, to rack of ears,
To moving on fours,

Where barks were language,
Where face explored for lack of hands,
I was this thing, and still,
Am what the death is now,

What the transmutation to not life
Has become, though still pound on,
Still dizzily speed, not flagged,
Now breathe for two, maintain, contain, retain
In you.

(2005)

What Desire Brings

All value lies within the heart
We steer the senses to,
And govern what the quality
Within our grasp depend.

It is the leaning out to reach,
To clutch beyond ourselves,
It seems a missing part extending
Where the beauty lie.

Where the best of ourselves
Connect to other things,
The balm of being smooth in grasping
What desire brings.

(2008)

Missed Opportunity

Without notice, silent destruction,
Missed opportunity like fetid shapes
Lingering, which could have lived,
Their faces close as fists I knew as child.

Now are bedtime mates which sleep beneath me,
Like warm pillows on tropic nights
Their hot breaths cross my face,
Which are my replacement for a kiss.

That entry which pulls up feral lust,
That opening to depths, that wound,
That slasher of sound that burns unseen scars
Extended to me searing balm.

Punching desire, gorged blood cock with a slap,
Pulling down hesitation I stand there ready
To be forgiven my fear of pushing off in darkness
To him, to his clamor for man touch,

For his aching energy, shy exposure of him,
Pallid skin uncolored by sunlight,
Like waxed pale fruit, he misses his prize,
Too late, steps away, unnoticing.

(2005)

Fists of Diamonds

It was in a sudden moment that he came,
And I had years of moments to give
Which were left emptied, like decay,
And rotted to the ground.

I had so long forgotten touch.
The isolation was a childhood of dark,
And his light was unexplainable,
As if the first time eyes could see.

For him it was illumination once again,
For me the first light I had known
And struck like fists of diamonds that were dirt before,
And pierced me, as I had them in my hands.

His foot touched mine, his eyes were bright,
His body was hard as we embraced,
And he was gone,
And I had altered, knowing there was light.

I had felt day, from night, upon my skin.
I had known changes in the dampness of the air,
And had enjoyed the warmth before he came,
But I had never seen the sun.

(2002)

The Drought

The drought is constant in its maintenance of dry.
Becomes like air we do not notice
When the breath extends itself, a millionth time,
Soft, invisible.

Like boundaries we do not feel, or touch,
Yet so powerful in us, reaching the depths of us,
As core of our unthought of self,
That regulate the need of wet.

This dust like thing, somehow surviving
With a memory of dew,
Appendage to intake the wet like some stone idol
That we worship as a link to having drunk.

We live as an arid thing, until the damp
Return the hunger of an oceaness,
A new parch in longing for the wave
Of it, then not as able to be thankful
For the mist.

Riker

Upon soft pillows lie, steady beast,
My own in keeping.
Here, strange fellows held in trust,
We join alone in touch.

Your scent is of the woodland,
Of dens, dry and dark,
And it is how I know you,
Deep musk moving into me.

Speak old child of woods, once
Where sires grew unknown of man,
And had no language there to share,
To comprehend that I could be.

Yet you were taken from them,
And lain upon me, as parent and lover,
I knew your firmness, as you delighted
To find in this new world, such bounty,
Such freedom from necessity.

It is here, years since we were just close,
That I have come to find you grown
Into a form of fur, and claw,
Developed so unlike me,

Though we are still bound.
And through dark remain,
Needing through our differences,
To hold each other warm.

(2002)

Brimming Flesh

Brimming flesh, my mated eyes
Put you into me, though we have
Never held each other close,
Though it is not for me

That you move, your pleasures
Are like scented smoke,
Like wisps of sultry ether,
Infecting without symptom.

Here, unguarded need enfolds you.
Hunger, out of some habit denied,
Burns again, though its food is illusion,
The satiation sparks at its return.

(2002)

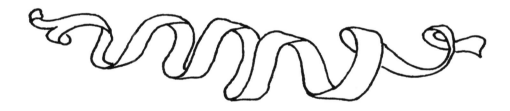

The Place, Of Past

I would not know the place, of past,
Its boundary is dim, like homeland mists
Across heather bogs ancestors knew,
Is lost, like they are lost from touch.

What speculation, to have been there once,
Fresh bodied stimulation, flesh formed
Again, the scenery, some incidental
Placing, for our eyes were only on ourselves.

And we were what was intended from bodies
To be close, were complete,
The air was immaterial, light only a source
To feel our senses within ourselves,

In hunger of touch, skin tanned firm,
Warm, sleek motion completed this creation
Of what we had desired to be,
Joined, thoughtless, composure drooling

Like fluid from our mouths, made glistening
On liquid seeming bodies caressing forms,
Not lingering to capture thought for memory,

We plunged, reckless, oneness down,
While day peaked, a slanting sun
Smoothing, silent, secreted us
By that marsh. Our sires

Had been there, gone as we are gone,
Now departed, traceless, damp, blowing,
Searing fog shrinks my skin,
As I awake, alone now, darkly shivering.

(2002)

Less Than Truth

The less than truth comes clear now,
Sharp in its attention, not the falseness
Like boy-men used to leave us
Out on roadways, to walk for miles

In the dark, because we were helpless once.
This is not quite sterling, but gives
The passer-by satisfaction that it is whole,
That we conform to his careless standards

Of affection. He does not anticipate honesty.
He does not recognize the near love,
The almost faith that passes for faith,
The scar that belies a festering.

It is the great illusion of sobriety.
To live, given the standard of human relationships
Without sincerity, to dream elsewhere,
To seek what is already at hand,

To live for that future that is already a past,
To look with eyes that are told what to see,
To punish more cruelly than fists,
Without touching, without concern, without restraint.

(2002)

Inner Self/Outer Self

5. Spiritual

A Destiny

So far from hope, that would I dare
To dream, the vision fail,
The almost grasp not now enough
To linger ages on its memory.

The somewhere land that must have been,
For I resemble in my life its form,
No longer known.
Its vacancy just centuries too long,
And I too weary to remember in the dark.

Yet to that course of lost eternity,
I turn myself forever like a lamp
That shine, regardless of the dark,
A destiny from oil that it knows not of.

(1977)

Higher Course

Their captains are asleep upon the bow,
And lights blink distant round the sea,
That mates may view upon a crest,
Or spy a star they gaze so constant,
And lift a higher course to them.

I hear the waters on the helm,
The hold is sunk in spray,
And visions round me dance in tempo to the gale,
And chant a prayerful tune.

(1976)

A Little Sea

To have a little sea,
Just big enough to sink,
To join the ancient fishes, in,
And grow a little gill,

And think in scales and darkness,
And hear the water sounds,
And climb into the deepest bottom,
And sleep until the light

Filter through, to resurrection come,
To rise upon that joyous day,
To burst into the air,
Like bubbles, crackling,

To feel the sweetness of the air,
To dry like silk into the breeze,
The magic day, the wholesome sight,
The mystic, maniacal delight!

(1976)

New Worship

He turned me in a finer hold
Than I have felt from deities,
And by his strange mortality
Would take my altar gifts.

But gods are vainer than the world,
And fickle as a drop of air
Goes any axis to new worship,
And any guarantee.

So to the simple prayers I turn
Again, upon my bended knee,
A pattern where to pray, is closest
That we come to faithful constancy.

(1976)

This Fortune

This fortune came as sweet as bliss,
Its footsteps in my room,
And I in wondering of eternity,
Seemed special to it, there.

I bowed, it sat, we thought alike,
Each captive to the space,
Where greatness, foreign in the outer landscape,
Came to rest.

We were so grand, the castles formed,
And we came spilling down,
Rubies in our pearls of diamond,
Satins woven lace.

Angels dipped in gold to see,
Their wings each color of the sky,
More beautiful than expectation,
Simpler than grace.

(1977)

New Consciousness

So close, like fear, like ships move
With all their compasses extinct,
We go into the shoals unaided,
By feeling past our thought.

And each long glide extend the dark,
So close to the source
Of hidden truth, just inability
To grasp, we agonize.

It grasp us, and as we horror,
In the touch of this unknown,
The purity of desire come,
And cleanse us, to new consciousness.

(1977)

We are as Madness

We are as madness still this equinox,
The moon is out of light,
And on her temples, empty in the cold,
We reach to, in our grasp.

We are the priestess of the brood!
Beyond the veil of passing, are again alight!
But this is another century,
So distant from the dynasties
Where we held every beam.

So foreign to the goddess live,
Her form is longing to be pleased,
And light her alabaster eyes with our holiness,
And walk amid the earth in stars.

I fumble in forgotten prayer,
I clutch my garments round,
Priest, priestess of my Isis from so long,
I awake!
I light the diamond fires up to you!

(1977)

Ancient in the Hills

Ancient in the hills, the temple stones
Lie ready as a sacrifice
To Goddesses, below our senses,
Wholesome in our hush.

Secret in their silences, they,
Who for a century are dim,
Then blaze into a magic starlight,
Crystal deep!

(1977)

This Great Machine

This great machine continue, though its purpose
Is unknown, as if some sense had not evolved
In it, some signal not designed in it,
Some direction not arranged.

It does not have the manual,
Nor required track, not rail, nor step,
Not surfaced causeway or path,
Not a groove to extend it.

It is without some plan.
Great holy houses churn to rectify it,
Their tomes of guidance, inner roads,
Their stern judgements

Bridle and halter, their blinders
That the journey they initiate
Not startle, their saddle padded, in promise
That their ride will ease.

Their sounds rise up like wind,
Their effect like fashions enwrap us,
Their sight, like flags shaken at us,
Surround us, abound at us.

(2008)

It was as Magic

It was as magic as a night
Upon the moon stone hill,
And we amassing at our forces,
Greater and greater still!

Until there was no thought of stop,
The power, like an edge,
Where we could see eternal blessing,
And blessing, and blessing still.

And each to hold on in the dark,
Our mind as close to burst, as burst,
Sensibility just thinking
Where we were, but we were gone!

(1977)

The New Reign

The red moon, bloated like a madness,
Is silent, as her spirits tremble
At the new reign of thought,
Her silver, glimmering in shadow, now.

Her space in sky no longer magical,
Its being form a different space
Where she may revolve as just a satellite,
Majesty unhooked.

Like blood gowns floating down to us,
Her beams all fitting that we easily put on,
And feel a tightening,
As we turn to our fleshy earth.

And form silent terrors that we know,
Like snakes around us dripping
In their venom, each life giving sting in this society,
To make us real.

`(1977)

Like Particle of Light

Like particles of light spread
One eon, down into this room of day,
To find me blissed upon religion bed,
I am waiting for the lily touch.

And rise at such secret splendor, now,
In wombfulls there of grace, and gain,
And specialness, and thought
Of what I have become to be.

Around me break the goodness, hark!
The glorified angels spreading in a move,
At proof I am divine, or they,
And lingering at glory.

Oh holy spot, to gain the be,
I am embodiment of it to you,
And sweetly bloom this quality,
This field, a flower stand

Redeemed, immortal, kneels on the land.
I rise as if the day bend down,
And arc me toward the sun, I linger
Sightward as I gaze on high
To grand illusion in the sky.

Survivor of the Place

I am survivor of the place,
That long ago had gone to dust
Like a vintage age.
I find some trinket of its having been,
And try to grasp some foreign memory
Of when I was a part of it.

I am as if I did not come from there,
The great age is done
That held me close, like mothers,
Though the memory is dim.

And if I live, it is the same to me
That such a land is where I am not,
And I can last without it, then,
And manage on invisible.

And at the end, a fulfillment come,
That to me, it must be like eyes, and strength,
That can somehow remember
Where I have been from,
And make the palaces again.

To be Grand

It is no consolation to be grand,
The trees are taller than I am,
The ground is older than myself,
Or so I may believe.

To be worshipped by the wind,
It would worship just itself,
If there was nothing else to touch,
And nature, so complete.

But to some hidden need,
The grandness might be big enough to touch,
And like a scent from butterflies,
The hidden boy may lift his head,

And turn in the direction of the source.
And there may be more than a wandering
Through life, somehow the webs of grand contain
A source of what the longing need for light.

(1979)

The Forest

The forest is ablack this consciousness,
Not seeming like a forest that we knew,
Its boughs unreaching, pathless form,
Like dark, we colorless expose.

We cannot reach it with our conscious selves,
As if bound by the words we put,
Only allows us an observation of the thing,
And limits it to halting thought.

We are constricted by our sense of self,
A form that cannot bear the flow,
So to it calculate from stiff propriety,
On frozen formulations of ourselves.

And to the monumentous gift of life,
We worship at a fruitless faith,
While like a hungered child, condition
All the ways to call for food.

(1979)

To be Powerful

A yearning to be powerful extends itself,
Called consciousness,
Its grasp is the furtherest reaches of the firmament,
For plan, or expectations.

The few, called by chance who
Rise like currents
From the imperfected masses,
Lure them with a promise, for a price,

Of extended ease and flow
Throughout their lives
Where they stumble, dim illumination
For direction in the blighted dark.

There are few destinies of anything else besides this scene.
Except at enlightenment, it seems
A permanence come to us of the thing,
We reach beyond the whisperings of dull sense.

There is a Pattern

There is a pattern seasons know
Like planets turning round a sun
Towards destiny of revolution,
Round itself in form.

As if the nature to the thing
Evolved some ability, like luminescence,
To attract worshippers
Of sun, who turn themselves in orbit,

And circle in their lives
About the force of warmth
They feel, as endless gravity,
And balance, harmonize their path.

The Dream of Life

To the dream of life I come,
Awake and mindful,
Of the fragile thing, its condition
Like the action of some primeval function,

Never understood, some thing
Which drives the masses to an unknown destiny,
As if an uncertain fate
Lie awakening at being grown.

I find myself adult in form,
Fashioned to a seamless regularity,
Each senseless act continue in a pattern
On itself, somehow becoming

What my grandsires had become,
And find sacrificed in the roar of survival,
Any mystic purpose, this life, it seemed,
Was evolved to signify.

Overhead

I'm going, too,
You promised,
That's all, that, I'm sure, of,
The gift waving, overhead,
I'll take!

(1968)

Simple Play

If Sunday's sweet, more often came,
To signal, simple, play,
To vaulted heavens, calling upon
Tiny feet,

Allowing psalm of jumping rope,
With time of, choir boy,
Easier stayed, our moments, then,
When friendly heavens, play.

When Day's About

When day's, about,
And I'm around,
I think of islands, in the sea,
And count how many live there,
And how many remember, me.

Land is only, solid,
For toe who needs the ground,
Someday maybe I'll report,
We've landed, Sir.

(1968)

Caretaker Candle

Caretaker candle, we're so cold,
And you so little, if only
Weren't the world so big,
And lifetime, take so long.

We don't need, surely, double pairs,
Of shoes to walk the, place we do,
And wait such hours for the bush,
To bloom, or bear a fruit.

Why, we'll just start out, getting used
To, how the fields and needle pine
Bend so, then get taken further
To a mountain, or a clime.

And in the dim of this expanse,
We hear the chapel bell,
A warning, to the lives that enter,
Will founder on the reefs of hell.

(1970)

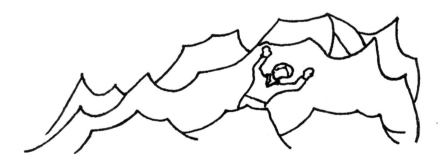

In Spite of Paradise

In spite of paradise, we are,
In spite of sacrament,
The tree comes out to bear a leaf,
And show off, to a friend.

Uninspired, in the heavens,
All the globes are on,
Waiting up, for God the Holy,
Showing Him they can.

Though He uses, all the earth
To tell He's still above,
We find a berry, and a second,
To sneak, surviving on.

While monuments appear in glory,
We lift our heads to cry,
And wonder why it sounds like singing,
Holy Jesus, Blest on High.

(1969)

He, and Angels

He, and angels by degree,
Go limitless intact.
Reelers of a rhyme and passion,
Silent, from simplicity.

Ancient to the age of day,
Bears reminisce of sky,
Opal as the sea in mixing
Ocean to the air.

I send him qualities of sky,
With tufts of Oriole,
And mix an ocean bred of ether,
Magic holiness.

The House of Marble Glass

The castle place, the good,
The house of marble glass,
Spreading, sends the hungry, gasping,
To breathe less often, saving air,

In piety. Destruction guarantee,
In this old building, like a darkness grew,
Balanced on a point of landscape,
That once the forests knew.

(1971)

I Brought My Jewels

I brought my jewels, to the Lord,
But he was not at home,
And angel too busy at some fortress
To take a note, I'd been.

And cold was everywhere, that day,
The sun was out of sight,
And world, for travelers, exacting
Fortitude, expense!

(1971)

Their Useless Wings

In Holy days there was the One,
Who spoke that all, could hear,
Language vast, when He was summoned,
Explaining just what could become.

And hallowed was the ground,
And simple was the Way,
That heaven was a lot, for Keeping,
Of distant ownership.

And all the pilgrims went abroad,
To learn with lesser things,
The power of Their useless Wings,
When everything could fly.

Just Eternity

I linked my coins, to a fist,
And hid them out of sight,
Knowing I could never, spend them
Unless to buy the world.

We went in Gold bazaars, imported,
From an ancient land,
Bargaining with Jewels, and Velvet,
Acres, for a glance.

Until upon a booth,
There was a Guarantee,
For just a Penny, and a Future,
And Just eternity.

(1973)

Some Say They Die

Some say they Die,
But I suppose, It is no greater thing,
Than Just a moment, of Refusal,
And then a, letting in.

Some Say they have not seen His, face,
And though I can not care,
Tell them He is just the same,
As Heaven, or despair.

And when I see my form, fast sleeping,
With dreams it tries to, speak,
There is no moment than the soonest,
To dream along with it.

A Holy Place

They took me to a Holy place
And bent my childish knees,
Pointing towards the East, a message,
Printed in the Wall.

I could not read, the Silence lagged,
Each letter was the Greatest chore,
So held my beads, kept fast, for keeping
Safe from any harm.

And thought I could not perish there,
In such a greatest house,
With windows for a Giant, peeking,
And incense in my eye.

(1973)

To Find This Ruin

It hurt me so to find this Ruin,
When I had no Balm,
And was hurried to the village,
On mission for a friend.

I stopped then, quietly, at the thing,
And raced my mind to see,
All the suffer at an instant,
And logic for it to be.

Whether He had climbed, too high,
Or leaned out on a Ledge,
Fallen with the heights and landscapes,
By such a narrow road.

I could not pass except to touch
The brow, and brush a thorn,
And gazed for just a moment, down,
But he had turned his head.

(1973)

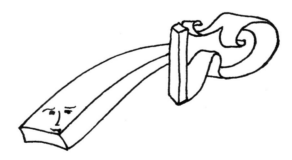

To Gloom

To gloom, salute I, dearest friend,
I fear eternity,
For just another age of wasting,
And talent borrow.

To throw there quickly, then be done,
When they shall ask what has been done,
Plead "Bankrupt" sir, I've not a penny,
And not an age to give.

For lain myself here to wish the thing,
Of majesty above,
And shake my fate at their cool judgment
With "this is what I've done" and been.

(1973)

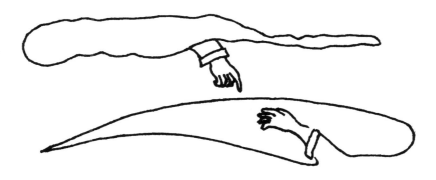

They Are Afoot

I have been from the mountain where all gods convene,
Their sparkled presence known,
Their scholarly benevolence adjusted to me,
Their kindly judgement shown.

They are afoot, these beasts of air,
These glorified exhibitors of sense,
Who dally soft among us, speak,
And foundations tremble, stones respond.

Hopes are given, guidance spread,
Balms of light extend,
They are conditioners of heart, seers of sobriety,
Robed things, old, bold things,

Which appear to have achieved what can be done,
Remind us that we are not big enough,
Not whole, not bright, not right,
Not extended, quite enough, to them.

Not excited enough, not one,
Not visionary, uptight, a sight!
We are on lower levels spent.
We are existing hell bent – a blight!

Such confusing delight,
Such senseless trails ignite,
Partitions push, muddled thoughts to fight,
Is this a waking dream? Goodnight!

(2006)

Paradise

Could this have been the paradise?
There are the remnants of a place
To which in minds aspire,
To which what is called hearts, desire,

To move upon this place,
In freshest morning awake
As creature footed, wing, or fur,
Or mineral in liquid, pour

Along rocked channel sound,
The music still intact in this paradise,
Though now is protected at the gate,
Like Eden lost.

This is the home man have bereft
Who had fled, or died,
Or pushed away for progress, or convention bound,
And must be kept apart,

Who would contaminate the very thing
He once owned, had once naked been,
Natural in, had enhanced in being,
Who stains this very thing he was.

(2006)

Heart Core

There is a self that does not speak,
Not move, nor urge itself
Upon the day, the roarings of moment,
The shifting passages of be.

It is a silent observation, like
Pharaoh's statue gazing out
Upon an endless tract,
Whose power lie in quietness.

Whose force is presence,
Invisible, steady guiding form,
Great monolith of stone,
Heart core of consciousness.

(2006)

Old Man Waken into Paradise

Though grown still, old man waken
Into paradise, blasted through
To charred forms at clogged spring
Where some forgotten past remain.

That garden is my home, though lost,
I have not been upon the site this century.
It seems the wet black, spread
Out as fallen trees, is familiar
To some kindred that comes out of me.

We are not whole, till home.
Though grey mudded earth be the landscape,
Here, the path to foundations sunken in
Were our rooms.

The fog light a seeming clarity evoke
What is a comfort in our blooded eyes,
To have returned. This is where
The ancients lingered, who were me.

This once bowered citadel still possible
To enter, though it had been terrifying
To seek with busy mind, enters me
And no lament, and to rejoice is done.

(2005)

To Not Believe

To not believe is sudden faith.
Coarse blinders slip
And there is light, just sun,
Just what once was not ourselves
Now looking in, self to self.

We are survival bound,
As if there were the finding out to do,
As if desire led to more discovery,
We reach, not out, but in,

Till we have formed a room, now safe,
And gaze along the flatness of our sight.
Outside becomes the treasure, or the loss,
Though we are whole, we do not know

The entirety. If only we were held, or holding,
And could release our selves
As we have done belief, and sleep
In muscle arms, other senses spiking, now our eyes are closed.

(2003)

For Infinity

I miss my holy books, that read themselves to me,
In such soft words, and situations,
In preparation for infinity,
That I might go, somewhere.

So packed my dews, and folded webs,
That I could wear for clothes
In that place, the Good book told,
And bear a crown, not hard to put on.

And so I went, I thought to God,
At least the scenery changed,
And others going led me onward,
To brinks, and long paths in the Wood,

Till I seemed lost, and they, somewhere,
Could not answer cries,
From one so little, with all fortress
Upon his head, and chains, and lies.

(1973)

The Carriage was at Distance

The carriage was at distance gone,
And slight the view, and light.
We were just passing what could not have been
A home, so spare the landscape,

So foreign the place to comfort.
And were distracted by the mud,
Half frozen, great ruts like barren furrows
Twisting layered at slopes,

Where misformed branches marked this boundary
Of road, we stopped.
It was not the waiting,
Hope had not discouraged us to plan.

Not company, for long the isolation
Had decayed communication,
So we stopped, it seemed a duty
To be there.

Old road, where some had gotten through,
There were the marks of their moving,
Some had gone by this spot.
Though we could not remember why we came,

As if some reason did not signify,
Not escape, no preparation for the journey,
It was the only thing that we could do,
To move on, no different than our standing still.

(2002)

The Quality of Touch

The quality of touch betrays its need,
Not just any hand can satisfy,
Though each desire looked upon
Roars in senses, the inner sound

More hidden all the more it fills
From sight. To control is depths
Of need held only by immobile features
Trained by fear, the single restraint

That holds heart forces from the pleasure
Surfaces which part at violence.
The beauty unobtainable glitters smake-like
Through its promise of venom to be released

Should more than glance alert it.
Its illusion to satisfy is sharp.
Its exposure to the senses cloud as drug,
The real wanting to join the beauty and the mind.

(2005)

There is a Sound

There is a sound the soul makes,
When it is unwound,
Like springs of clocks when they are tightened
Past their boundary of tight.

And ever then the tick is out,
Like some gigantic shadow left,
And all the gears are forfeited
To silence, at a pause.

The form seem same,
There is no notice at the glass
Of what has done within,
Except the quieting.

And like us, just a lack of sound
Tells all the soul has been,
And with it we will never know the magnitude
Of loss, until our gauges run again.

(1978)

So This is Paradise

So this is paradise,
Come through, some silent place,
That I had not expected
Would find me here,

Where all depart familiarity,
With what I know,
Some welcome place,
Intended to reward, or praise,

Or mark some recognizable
Finality of the journeyer,
Or bear some noble aspiration
The voyager lean into.

This place of bliss,
This final home,
This mark of sensibility,
And excessive formulations of the place

Remain, at last, as beautiful
As that which had been lost,
Whose presence suddenly displaces
The need to enter in.

(1985)

An Opiate of Day

There is an opiate at day,
Which scientist deem sun,
We regulate to meet each dawning,
From some primeval, when

We fled the silence of a dark,
And with a mighty rise,
Push all the depths before us, lighted,
And search the remnant out,

Till we are brighter than a noon,
And yet, our pale, unceasing tread,
Seem dim to crystal palaces,
And bulbs of radiance.

We do not become the gift of light,
Our singular inability to illumine anything
Return us to the deepest,
And bright expose our shadow form.

(1986)

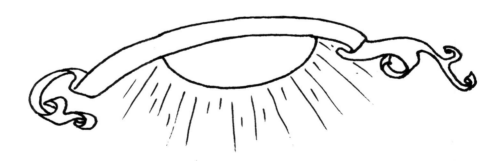

Not Far from Grace

We are not far from grace who stand alone,
In silent rapture of the day,
In still rooms where the moment
Is all there is of life.

And we are forgotten, no place in worlds
To cling where activity rules,
No home among the masses,
Whose lives are controlled by the noise they make.

There is no record here that we have been,
Whose growth like trees, is not noticed,
Till their great boughs shade over
Generations passed by with such effort,

Who never looked up,
So difficult were their lives.
But we effortlessly expand around them,
In a different sort of life.

Here, where perception of quiet fills us
Like snow covering us,
Like water suspending us,
Brings peace, and movement, like death, is done.

(2002)

The Light Is Just Upon Us

The light is just upon us now,
Familiar in its silence, and we are safe.
Come through here, having found sobriety,
Like passions stilled that we may breathe,

Without expectation, or plan.
Somehow having worn away the pleasures
We thought were possible through touch,
And desire, which had relieved us of an emptiness.

Come through now to this spot,
Where no waiting is done. No mansion house
To find, no brotherhood to redeem us,
Illusion burst suddenly.

This seeming wreck where we have stood
Is all there is of paradise.
No wings to lift us, no home,
No unity in human sympathy.

It was a drunken state, to feel.
The light is clear upon this legacy,
Our skin is bark, and branch reach out from us,
To express itself, which once were fingers
Clutching in the dark.

(2002)

Upon The Depths Of Paradise

We are upon the depths of paradise,
The old forsaken plain, where wind
Is the voice there, light its eyes,
Form its barren expanse,

Extending past our view.
It is not the promise we knew
In incense halls, not the home
Of Christmases we shared.

But something solitary, no heights
To overlook creation's spread,
No journey of salvation to achieve its land,
It is a destiny of survivors to be had.

Safe, upright, silent, we spread upon it.
Come through now, not of our making,
Not hope attains it, but final thing,
Should we live long enough

To grow into it, like sharp reality,
The presence of all belief decays,
Brittle pupa cracks, its jelled interior
Will suck the ether air of that stark place.

(2002)

This Almost Weary Bright

So this is paradise, old familiars glorified
Reach out with tendrils pointed in golden plate,
And pierce me, sweet nectar
In rising fog-like mists from turning censers.

It is abundance that has brought me here.
Calculations of effects, qualities of silent things
That can be placed admiringly
To lift me high and reach this place.

Longevity has induced it, trial endured,
The wounds are clad in laces to disguise their scar
And haul me to the station it seems
Is necessary to be held.

Here is the thing now brought to life.
Its stories can be whispered, though no sound
Can reach me here. It is the throne
Of harsh sobriety and opulence

That attract what glories come to me,
What happy cherubim alight
And cast me in such ray-like mornings,
And evenings grown colored, riotous

Without roar, I recognize the site,
So spark-like momentary lumination,
And here, the spark lingers to illume
This clarity, this solitude, this almost weary bright.

(2005)

Into Consciousness

I call myself into consciousness
For I am, before all things, I am.
I call from the dark, to dark,
To let be light, to warm the new me.

Let there be sound, that I may sing!
Let fleshy move, that feel such thing
As such I am, that I may dance!
See creation move in me.

And, oh to touch. Magic senses
That connect me to these things I am,
To reach out. To awake!
Joyful dawn, core of my sensuality self.

(2011)

There is a Place

There is a place of paradise
We recognize in dream,
A place as if interior, as home,
A feeling of content.

As if at young among the green,
Prismatic color of the sky,
And earth, enameled in its florid sheen,
Become a place of bliss.

One would think it heavenly.
It is a land of sense
Painted in a warmer vision
That striving can not give.

It is a freedom of movment, and space,
An intimacy of touch,
A timeless, painless, clear sensation,
We go to, deep within.

(2008)

The Sifting of Eternity

I am warm now, some internal heat renews,
Though I have lived for decades in search
Of external heat. Some desire must have mistaken
What appears to be illumination, but is reflection, of me.

Though this ability to sustain does not overwhelm,
It does not scorch. There is no sweat
In its mediocrity. It is not a sun.
It cannot burn the earth, or in abeyance freeze.

It steadies on and does not light enough to see
Beyond this small space, like old stars piercing
To this ground that already have gone out,
That have not finished being bright.

It is a private flame that does not share.
Bright in dark, loud in still,
Amost a friend in comfort where there are no friends,
Where the sifting of eternity is blessed.

(2005)

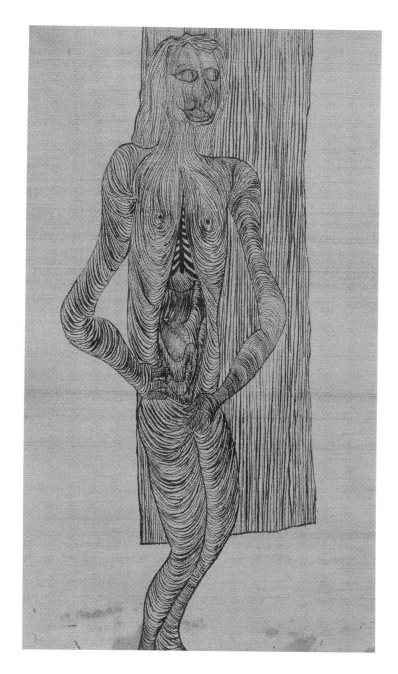

The Poet

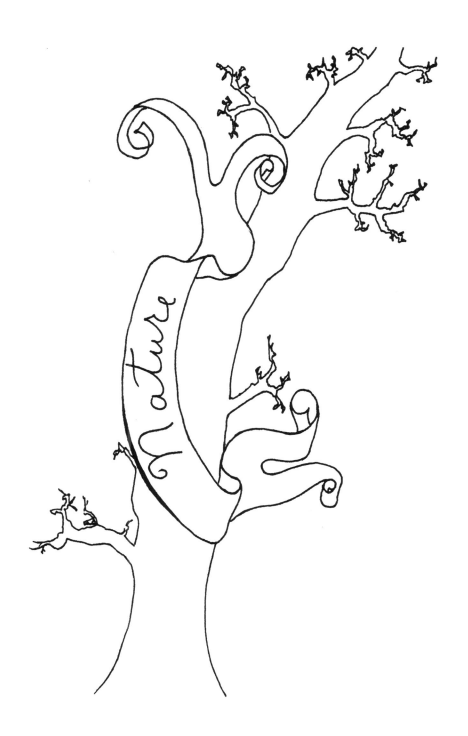

Nature

In the Spring

When I am stronger in the spring,
I'll touch the window sill,
And raise a tender head in wonder,
And take my fill.

The scent of air, the touch of balm,
The light etherial,
The monment pressing past all wonder,
The thing, material.

Unlike the drifting sense I hold,
Within this darkened space,
Its phantom citadels of gauze,
Its stately, painted face.

This freshing season will come clear,
Will sift euphoria,
Its light condition, warm in remission,
Will spark my cold interior.

(1994)

Since all the Woods were Sold

It has not been the same
Since all the woods were sold,
And we, pensioned in the city,
Are placed into a room.

And set to look out on the noise,
And fade into the streets,
And like a curtain, change to yellow
Because the air is dull.

No visions in this soil,
I waken in the faded light
And smell the forest memory,
As if I were the thing.

And dream almost of being safe,
Of having legions of the trees,
To hold all in their grasp of velvet,
And turn a danger out.

And bind with heavy needles,
And plait a simple den,
Lie softly in the air around me,
And hush a lifetime in.

(1978)

Cat

He is at self with nature,
This creature that we know,
Glide silent on some sinewed hinges,
Never following.

No tract is his, the mansions fail to contain him,
Possessions, only coat and pad,
And then occasional, some flurried creature
Cease itself at jaw.

And he continue like a day,
No thought except a sense of momentariness,
And to us, come judgmental of our noticing,
And give us form of our intent before we know.

(1979)

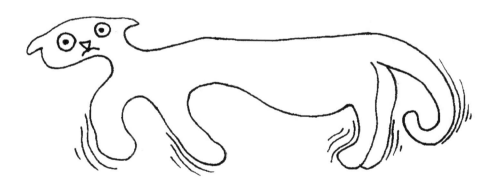

Nature's Breathing Form

We are abright, who are alert to nature's breathing form,
Its easy shape to recognize,
Come like a longing has ended,
Suddenly upon us.

As if the dull beyond the pain
Some drug relieve,
And quiet once again into us,
Can endure the day.

As if beginning, a new feeling thing,
Some other self become into us,
An unimagined freshness moving
To the brink of another consciousness,

Where primal beings upon the tree of this new life,
Their browned, moveless eyes,
Linked to nature thought,
Scan quick our newborn shape, glistening.

Habitat of Destiny

It is the silence that we come to know.
Some habitat of destiny,
Brought here in moments from a once ago
We think of at a pause,

As some antique remembering,
Of what it must have been
Upon the landscape of that wooded
Majesty of then.

To gird our footing at the land,
To blend among the glen,
And find a vastness in an acre
Where all ourself may stretch.

And all the freedom to be grand,
And all the space allowed,
Ability to own its holding,
And place it loud within.

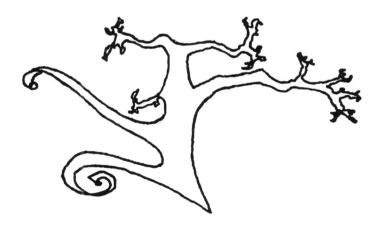

There is a Sound

There is a sound, that to a sense,
Come noticed all to nerve, and thought,
A movement in the wind
Awakening giant families of tree.

And then like whisper, that we know,
The limbs begin their voices, in reply,
And magnify themselves,
And speak so vaulted in the air.

Their language just as old as they,
Exclude us, till we listen with ourselves,
And hear, through faces and through hands,
And speak ourselves, unknowingly.

And then, when we are common
With the thing, a new sense
Come to us internally,
That gird us like the strength of this forest society.

(1978)

The Place

There is a place past wanting
That we long to reach,
To step through the helplessness
Of being left alone.

A place of cool woodlands,
Where once was home,
Whose determination was survival,
And peace was being part of everything.

Where danger was a clear distinction
To run, or fight upon,
Where desire ruled love,
Where mirrors were only drinking pools.

Yet we are past redeeming, from a wooded place.
Through curse or force of consciousness,
Stand isolated, finally, in wooden rooms,
On carved, dead trees, stretch out claws,

That grasp in stillness
For that place to come to us,
Where we are belonging,
Where we are whole again for what we used to be.

(2002)

The Sea is Up

The sea is up, her waves, arching,
Flap the shores in two,
And spell in ocean, sacred moments,
Messaged out of sand.

To come to read occasional,
The misty board the way,
And wrap extending fingers, lending,
Most inquisitive, a grasping plan.

They reach the mystic plain,
They tread and stimulate,
Expressors needing beached surroundings,
Camaraderie with such a view.

Stand, sterile, stark, upon the surf,
Their piercing eyes review
What passion surge, moving past them,
In nature's vast, unyielding roar.

(1971)

Misery Paints

Misery paints color, blending,
Confusing who she sees.
The bee on paper knowing petal,
Forgets himself in doubt.

What he had to qualify,
And keep a pact ago,
Descendant of the greater hives,
Is put without a heritage.

A Fiber of a Gem

The sun was highest at his peak,
And I stood up to see,
Calculating at my doorstep,
Beams, that floated down.

They seemed a fiber of a gem,
And easily displayed,
Monumental to the moment,
Of vast continuance.

All the Busy Green

I find no Royal, but an Inch,
And all the busy Green,
Sectioning in millimeters,
Joining, blade by blade.

And bowing to the air, in quarters,
As if in layers blew,
And covering within a landscape,
That only seconds know.

(1973)

Wilderness

We understand the Wilderness
Who are not wild,
And stolen are from Habitats,
Once mild.

Choose we cannot, to the Wood,
Where flow eternally our source,
Our job is some survival,
Our place, in hall or room,

And learn we do, and learn we well,
What life experience,
Instills into us like a shove,
The impermanence of place.

We Stand Up

We stand up, still, when we can stand,
Recovered, from a drought,
And notice that the woods, are older,
And taller than we are.

To see above the fir, and pine,
Oh, to see a crest,
And look beyond the boughs and branches,
Into another habitat.

Genuine the trees, undo,
When we are patient, long,
And show us what they've seen forever,
And seem to ask us what we know.

When They Call

Legions knock on rainy roof,
Beaconing me out.
Fireside looks careful now,
To see what I'm about.
Windows stick, and door ajamb,
Will tend my prison wall,
Longing hope seems louder here,
When they call.

(1969)

Pardon

Boxes of roses far away
Request a stem or two,
An angel treading silently
Today,
Requisitioned pardon
Of the lot.

(1967)

A Ghostly Costume

The town was silent, but Awake,
I rushed to see the view,
Captains in a ghostly costume,
Marching pace, by pace.

The moon was there, her light intact,
More paled the secret crew,
And through the place they softly murmured
Things I never knew.

I left my gaze and hurried Down,
To follow where they went,
But stood alone beside the pavement,
And watched the Moon, go out.

(1973)

I Am of Autumn

I am of autumn in this state,
And ever see the leaves and faded grass,
And nothing at all to do, but count them,
And think it is a harvest, today.

And dream of real harvests, when at child
I used to bind the barley, corn and wheat,
And dance green and golden,
Round the pumpkin piles,
And sing some apple tune, with all the trees.

I used to have so much to do,
Those days of increase, and bounty gain,
And satisfaction seemed in numbers,
We'd think each autumn was the best.

But then the months fused, one by one,
And whether it was day, no one told,
And silence spreading like a hush,
And no more canning jars to fill.

But I had loved too long, the fields,
And plucked this state of life, among the many,
And polish it, till I seem fading,
Becoming those sweetest, lost afternoons.

(1973)

Land Alive

It was as Years ago, the land alive,
And I in some estate,
Would wake upon the meadow blooming,
And trees, in State,

Would wag their fruitful heads, at good,
Unknowing, none of bad,
And touch eternity, at limits,
And sky be just of clouds.

And sweet was heaven, in our Midst,
The bounty, all for all,
To teach us nothing but perfection,
We could already teach.

And flow, the land and unity,
The paths unbridled, full,
And death an instant of refilling,
Then go unmoving, on.

(1973)

Infinity

I could not pry infinity,
So it unraveled down,
Sightless to the end of vision,
Unending tumbling.

To show me all its form, flew out,
Expanded cordially,
Marking skies of swirl, and fashion,
Painted majesty!

(1971)

Judy

She told me, that there was a sun,
And that I ought to see.
Running out among the trees,
Looking for her friend.

She showed me, just how round he was,
And where he usually goes,
By making patterns with her hands,
Drew where his sunbeams are.

She said he wasn't, far away,
Or very big at all,
And with her biggest laughter,
Said he did that, too.

She knew him well,
And all the places, where they used to sit,
Promised that she'd take me soon,
As long as three could fit.

(1969)

Taken Places

The summer fell, and left me jewels,
Ones, she, used to wear,
And now that, I've taken places,
I sit, in quieting,

With some old, autumn, for the daylight,
Some old fall, for night,
And with the rivers flowing through me,
Lull myself to sleep.

Adding up the World

The sun ran out of day, this week,
While adding up the world,
Stopping to adjust her trip,
To fit the bumpy, way.

She wasn't sure there'd be enough,
To feed the growing place,
So rationed sunbeams for the hoard,
Suffering in place.

(1969)

Nature Tempts

Nature tempts her Favorite children
With lands, they've never seen,
And offers as she gives her Bounty,
In veil and promises.

To teach or temper all her brood,
Gives part to every one,
And for herself, the key of ever,
To lock the Children out.

And make them bowers they may not Take,
And forests everywhere,
To punish, showers into Oceans,
And parch the Soul.

And they may learn, unflinching Pain,
And gain ability,
To regulate, and Concentrate,
And thank her for infinity.

(1973)

The Greatness

Before, the greatness stem from Summer,
And I upon its leafy head
Rode strong, as if at plant,
My nurture live in green delight,

And I was golden with seasons' lore.
The logic of my station, there,
Seemed simple, and the times were ancient,
For great trials to be overcome.

But all I knew, that we were stable,
And on the spring and Autumn rode,
Till frozen, Just the grief survived,
Alone, my winter paramour.

(1973)

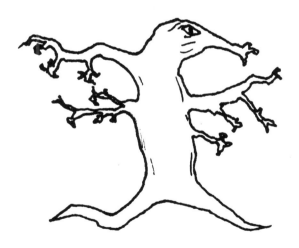

Earth and Air

Better to be reached by earth,
Than reach the air and try to hold
Its willing breeze and nature blessing,
To try the cloud-formed bed in nuptials of hymn.

And hymenaeus sing his long forgotten melodies,
And birds as bridesmaids round the door
To greet conception with a flight,
And seasons all their gifts to spread.

Awaiting with the morn the married pair,
All in the chamber hidden, grasping,
Air to flesh, and flesh to air,
Yet phony rise to spread their bloodless sheets

In shame that they had never touched,
Though willing, they had never breached
The citadel to pleasure, at being one,
And must deny their want, annul their main intent.

And earth alone await, in time it prosper,
Faithful lover of fleshy brew,
That never jealousy inhabit, patient mate,
In silence hold its form upon itself.

There conception rights itself,
And earth entwine her sodden, loving arms
About the form, and bit by atom, join
The pair forever in its musky sacrament,

Till they are one, and air continue
To be tried by those who think they can,
And spend their life in courting,
Till earth takes them home,
Enshrouded in her soft eternity.

(1974)

Sometimes in the Still

Sometimes in the still, I see
The carriages of glaze advance,
Their wheels of ether on the firmament,
Turning by the sun.

And ladies dripped in satin lace,
Each finger round a jewel,
Pointing at the forest, swept in alabaster,
Mists and golden ribbons at the air.

As if they were the guardians
That sign each perfect thing,
And check it in its royal latitude,
And spins it into place.

And just as I began to speak,
The sky on pinions fled,
And tipped a casket of its diamonds
On my head, in rain.

And all the majesty consumed,
It melted out of sight,
And left me shivering in memory,
Of what so close, had been.

(1975)

Out of Deep

Out of deep lain forests crept the sluggish form,
Anxious to inflict upon the meadow in the light,
His shedding body, with a hoard of followers
They came, so many from the dark.

And settled in their needs to leave the cold,
Wrapt mighty on the hardened land
To strive, without the forest for their home,
And build strange avenues to fit themselves.

From this factory of place we have evolved,
Forgotten of agos, we languish at our bones
Some moments, when we find stiff prints
Unlike our own, and terrible to touch.

And know it was the monster that had left
His steel rememberances,
And like a trap for centuries,
We nibble on the food, unthinking yet all knowing,
That he will return, and snap our bulging cheeks.

(1975)

Sufficient

It's sufficient,
Thou who gives with bounty,
All that remains to, lack,
Is necessity.

I don't need a, million, miles
To walk along, gardens,
A day of fall, and breath,
Will be enough.

Garden's Hue

Petal's nice
To make a rose,
Request a, Bee, for glue.
Slender touch will, hold it,
For, stem,
Roots are not required though,
In spring,
In mystic garden's hue.

The Thing

How easy to be senseless brought
Into the firmament,
To be the thing the senses fathom,
To be the little stone.

To be the plainest form of all,
To be the lump on earth,
That comes and goes within a movement,
And is forgotten, or unfound.

Yet to build, and pile, and regulate,
Other grasping creatures live,
And after they have all gone out,
The earth return to still.

(1976)

The Greens

The greens had shred into myself,
And made me special to the autumn sounds,
And I spun silvers like a web,
And caught at air, and tugged at dew,

And fed on spaces round the drops,
And knew each particle of foresting,
It was like all the world come out
To shine a harvest day.

Like wreaths of color filled with scents,
So rich, an earth size gem abound,
And melt into me as communion,
I was big enough to take.

And I was glorious, in this span
The solar systems knew,
And lifted me like a flash of lightning,
Now still can smell the ozone burn,
For a remembrance.

(1978)

Nature's Desire

[437]

7. Home

The Place We Have Come From

This is the place we have come from,
We know it by the form it had,
That memory allow, empty, beaten halls
That crowd with still formed ghosts.

Their eyes are not upon us now,
Pacing, in some old routine of move,
They form a spectral band,
Where they appear to congregate.

Returning there, we cannot go,
The journey takes too long for life,
To reach into the hideaways of then,
It is a different place than light.

And senses do not feel,
Yet to turn away from their dim sightings,
To those blurred expanses,
Becomes stopless loneliness.

Family - 1

There is a place you cannot go,
For wanting shies the thing from grasp,
And hope denies it from yourself,
And faith must fail you finally,

Of that fair land called home.
That is a thing each creature knows,
That is the point where they begin,
And only know it when they are the closest

To its memory. Of family, that does not
Require day, that light would only burn
The sweet arms reaching to the self,
That to hold, is all each being need.

That there, in touch we may embrace ourselves,
No judgment come, no spectral, darkened angels hovering,
This is the place where we are joined,
Into each other, naked, finally.

(2000)

Family - 2

There is a place you cannot go,
For wanting shies the thing from grasp,
And hope denies it from yourself,
And faith must fail you finally,

Of that fair land called home.
That is a thing each creature knows,
That is the point where they begin,
And only know it when they are the closest

To its memory. Of family, that does not
Require day, that light would only burn
The sweet arms reaching to the self,
That to hold, is all each being need.

It is a place you cannot part,
Its lure unmoved by worldly thing,
We sit enshrined one day in splendor,
Yet stand on footing of childhood play,

Move carelessly in noonlight circle,
Brave seas of ceaseless roar,
Expand until our senses crumble,
Yet touch the thing no more.

Within the Darkness

Within the darkness come a tug,
A longing to be gone
To home, to forests, dusty waysides,
Toward the place we have been from.

Where all our memories point toward,
Where we were at peace, it seems,
The smaller that we were,
The closer to the quieting.

Yet to the place is blocked in time,
Our habitats are done,
And yearning turn upon itself in inability,
To move, and change into a loneliness.

We balm with action so it cannot feel,
Until addicted to the motion like a drug,
Replaces possibility of other homes,
Yet gives a hope we will arrive.

(1980)

As if the Age had Stopped

As if the age had stopped within,
And this still room as testament of when
The sounding silence came upon
The artifacts of day,

A calm was amid the form.
Upon the hold of sense it lay,
Now gentle habitation
With the memory of once ago,

That led it to this spot of quiet,
The hand now groping on itself
For sustenance, no longer reaching out
In the dark, but to the self.

A smaller hold, though ageless,
As the journey in life
That had been a dream,
To this pilgrim, for a land of home.

The Urge of Home

I lean in towards the urge of home.
What is this place, old homestead fair,
Enshrouded, coming from mists to light,
Unlike the day, some other luminescence shine?

It is the place of welcoming,
The worn, familiar thing, the place
Where spectral arms advancing,
To take a person in.

To reach it they must have been afar
For these to know the land,
For those to seek the comfort, waiting,
That slips beyond the hand.

That does not pale at touch,
That does not fade at sight,
That streams beyond the expectation
Minds put up, who are too grand.

It is the cool simplicity,
It is the fresh, from common thing,
Which make the stones a diamond setting,
Which make desire, gently sing.

(2008)

Had I Just Waited

Had I just waited at the day,
But clock was past the noon,
And somewhere in the hills a longing to me came,
And I listened at the door.

And quiet as the sound, I fled,
The streets were night like dim,
And as a shadow in them formed myself,
Away, forgetting where I had been from.

And what the loss? No one at home
To answer for the majesty,
Who each one lifetime, comes in courting,
For those that stay for him.

(1976)

The Memories

I know it, by the memories
It gave me at the time,
And put them in an airy box,
Stored behind my room.

When night up, fills the empty air,
I check them one by one,
And add a little from a thought,
Which seems to take me home.

The Terror House

It seems the terror house is still.
The silence of it come
And bode me like a memory
About to recreate.

About to reinstate its pain,
About to grip me round,
And send its fingers far in to me,
And pull an agony.

And choke a scream, so deep within
That would the volume show,
No destiny could pass beyond it
Like storms the oceans throw.

(1978)

My Homely Habitats

My homely habitats are done,
The wood is brittle dry,
And though the sun is on horizon,
It burns the simple place.

My only home is crumbled, down,
And at the wreckage place,
I lie upon the darkened fortress,
And touch it with myself.

(1973)

That Land We Dream

Oh, to that land we dream to go,
In frigates, or across some mountain steep,
Climb onward, safe our journey through,
The compass always pointing noon.

The day awake, and we are well,
And on to hope and happiness,
Always arriving at each step,
Into, and from our mansions at the sea.

So blended that the floors are liquid
To the stair of mountain bliss,
To climb each night in worldly expectation,
And find the linen neat.

(1976)

A Habit

There is a habit in the form,
Which lingers like the memory,
Of grand, some golden idol
The inheritance poor descendents contemplate.

It calls, its plump lips
Form sweet images toward the little self,
Of superior appearances of importance,
Whispered silently like a balm

Upon the human condition. It appears
It could give the whole of life purpose
Of comfort midst darkenings of trial,
Of tiresome fate,

(continued)

Of being herdlike treated by cruel destiny.
O come! Soothe us like the fashions
Our ancestors wrapped upon themselves,
In silk, and pearl, and home.

(1981)

The Solitary

There is a place the solitary know,
Like an old estate where ancient
Beings who once inhabited,
Left tomblike shadows that they had been there.

Its parlors are a colorless dream,
Each stone fast particle of stationary form
Contain momentous regulation
For the self to gird upon.

And put a plan away, quiet the only vision
In the still to grasp,
The oaken doors firm against unknown invisibles,
Hiding all within.

An isolated, damp interior,
And sense lie stark by intensity,
We freeze into the mansion like a voyager
Who only wished to voyage home.

(1981)

Once by Paradise

Some dial within the form point home,
A constant beacon set some eon,
Once by paradise where happy beings
Stood within the spot.

And sense must have been within,
No vision necessary, being whole,
In an unconscious spun eternity of calm,
The living elements in place.

Yet like awakening to cinder gowns,
Our vision in the cold of light
Keep strong the waiting search.
We press each particle of memory to find

Some distance thing, now lost,
As if the feeling that the majesty had been
Upon us,
And faded to a mist of something dim.

(1981)

The Stilling

The stilling in the brain contain
A lessening of view,
Of striving round the outer door,
To present happenstance.

Some click dissolve the steady reach,
Its silent grasp upon the day release,
And turn into the room
Some ancient left as testament.

Their once agos superior resolve,
To fit among the bodices of them,
And deep into the oaken station,
Close the door within.

And wait, somehow conditioned to the spot,
Its form more lovely than we know,
And willing to contain another voyager,
We come as close to home within,
As memory allow.

(1981)

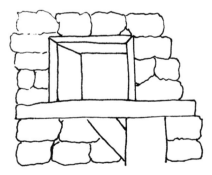

A Silenced Thing

The passing of a silenced thing,
Is often all I know of its once
Having urged me into Zanzibars,
And unknown foreign lands of chance.

As if some journey defect made
The passage obsolete, and where
I had been going, now tender
Vague collections of a memory,

That to its essence linger,
For some remembrance of why
I had continued out so long,
For some condition, or sure meeting

Of a greater happiness, some need so
Greater than my home
Could have meant for me.
Its passion must have been greatest

To consume me, now longing
To become again the thing, each particle
Of me return to, formlessly,
To that lost place, once paradise.

(1982)

Troubled Things

Outside this room lies troubled things,
I barely dare to venture, thinking to go,
Like running in darkness,
The sensation of the contemplation

Great enough without the act.
Though with the passing of my innocence
I am aware of an exterior
From my playhouse room, a hatch

Where I may pass into unknowingness,
Out there where rust blood skies
Hold scudding strips of filthy rag clouds
Over orange parched, charred tree, dotted,

Barren hillsides that extend beyond my comprehension,
I may go. I may extend a visitation
To this other place that in my consciousness
Is there, beyond my measued, detailed walls.

That is an outside from my in,
A going from my staying to be here,
Like Eden must have been beyond the fall,
Another place that this is not.

Where such unlikely spaces span,
To not be here would be a plan
I would in fact, delay the thought
To be somewhere, where I now, am not.

(2007)

The Verge of Fate

Leaning on the verge of fate,
Old past entwine with now,
Its grey head youthful in a memory,
Its then brought sharp

To one last salutation in the dark,
One last possibility of touch,
One life still motioned on this plane
Of now, still stationed at the door.

At journey's length, that thought of den,
That knowing in the world it was,
Was compass in a rotted landscape,

Sobriety, in madness burned in heat.
It was the hinge that kept the door,
The light, though blinded such ago,
Came soft as if there were no need for eyes.

And this is at the moment of its loss.
Where long extremities will patient spread
The brittle dimming of the faded memory,
It now contains, its grasp,

Though continents apart, still there,
Its form, still moving at an edge
Which shall extinguish like a snap,
And cease the heritage of home.

(2007)

On to Consciousness

The beast strive on to consciousness,
Its misformed outer self evolve
From inner workings, slow mutations
Of unknown urging, aching on

To guide the primal, wary thing
From dens it stationed home,
From clime it grew a part of,
Of community of wildwood habitat,

Till it reflect upon itself,
Its power shift to dream imaginings
Of spectral dark, to near invisibles
Of other forms beyond its sense of scope,

Till it look out beyond its reach,
It sinewed neck raised up
Into another darkness, other mystery
Of outer being that it cannot touch.

It feel at last a longing, first emotion
From a warm haze, to isolation,
Stark as its first pain, first shivering,
First clarity of its destiny of loneliness.

(2007)

Dark Child

Rise up, rise up, dark child,
The circled moon is fading
Past the hazed circumference of sky,
The grey infinity of light is circling

Round as if a dampness weighted it to earth,
Spreading to the firmament,
The silence of its movement
Like some stealth beast, suddenly awake,
And upon the day.

It is the destiny of this shy perception
To inhabit such a mystery
Of dull illumination, past the weight
And sweet embracing of Morpheus,

To step upon the habitat of station,
Gird the slight awakening
Of some lost purpose of some once plan
Of daring being, some lingering possibility

Of great awareness, now slipped
Into antiquity, living artifact of once when,
Templed then, now still peering out
As some worn statue on a flattened plane.

(2007)

Homeland

There is a place we cannot find,
Cannot reach at clime,
Though artifact remain, and trinket lure,
Their hint sublime of this lost paradise,

We cannot go. Its lands were once,
Its cottage, citadel, remembering
From childhood lingering at mind,
Some century ago at life.

Surrounded by its magnitude,
Increased by age, enchanted by loss,
As it contain a source of us,
A gauge as compass,

A touch of gentle hand, a face
In shadow, dim the recognition
Of its silent form, soft the stillness
Of its blurred embrace.

It was a thing of hallowed place,
A sweet belonging to,
A destiny, reversed in passing scope,
That finally end where we began.

(2007)

Not Home

This is not home, though I have lived here endlessly,
I have become this place.
Dreamed of it, though I now dream,
It is a vapor I inhale.

It is a memory that I live, not awake,
Though I move in clarity, and step
Lightly as if familiar paths lead
To new places, but I have travelled them,

And in circle come around again.
This is not the place of what I am,
Though I contain it, I extend it into being,
My presence form it, enliven it.

I had sought here wholeness, touch,
Though what can touch me is only myself.
I longed for being other than Me,
But here is only particles of self.

I do not despair it, not pause in wandering
Among it, though it cease to mystify,
It is a plane of sensuous compassion,
Where I pause to know myself.

(2006)

Home

All things lean towards what is home,
Though must imagine such a place,
So undefinable, is daily sought,
Yet no foundation can maintain.

No dwelling last beyond the life,
No nest support the hatchlings grown,
No bower stand as seasons flow,
Though precious, far beyond their form.

It is what holds the steady course,
What lingers when the course is gone,
What compels in memory to site a spot
Where moments reached a hope of it.

It cannot fade, though all decay,
The rubble transmutate in newer form,
That reach out where the old had been,
To linger there again.

And all say home, show gods and citadel,
Prove through holy books, ignite in word,
Form in statute, pass law to judge,
Guide through ruts of century.

The place just out of sight
That all desire toward, though cannot reach
At life. The spangled carnival of noise
Forget the quiet silence of our core.

(2006)

Child's Estate

I have seen the spot of home,
Its place now marked in view,
Is where I keep my last possession
Of a child's estate.

Its road is not too far from here,
Its shape beyond the hill,
And just an afternoon to find it,
And just a pleasant try.

To be again where I have been,
The place all aspiration bring,
And lifetime leaning for the moment,
To be there.

And yet a lingering within, to realize,
A hunger pressed against the thought of satiation,
Is but the only compass and attraction,
The only guide I know.

So stand upon the mount of vision
To this old paradise,
And stay, in cold sobriety of longing,
To keep the clarity of sight.

Generations Ark

I am a generations ark,
Their voiceless once agos
Melt into me now, some unintended heritage,
Passed in by giving need.

Some movement added to the brain,
Extensions from an ancient self to self,
That make the solitary more,
The empty framed at full,

The character set upon the mind,
Some stable area,
We lean into as age dissolve us,
From this momentary residence of home.

This Place at Last

We have come to this place at last,
A final destiny,
Though unaware we were to travel,
When we were home.

Some unseen movement, at the first,
Discomfort at the brain,
A lingering to find those kindred ones,
Who were gone from the place we had come from.

And now the ache itself is done,
And we are foreign still,
Though far from any family,
We had a dream to know.

Self Portrait

8. Later Poems

The Moment

The moment is forever on this earthly sill.
A gift from gods who finger galaxies
And count the grasses at an inch,
The one inheritance we grasp

In our dim and fading stumble
Called life, our choke of clarity
Amid the roar, the blacking span
Before oblivion enclose us like a hush.

The instant is a balm no drug could match,
A sense of paradise,
A scent of perfumed vapors wafting high
Upon the ruined form,

Whose sensibilities crack brittle
On the waste of hope for touch,
The useless strive for home,
A trinket of familiarity

Amid the shifting vague diversions
That blinder possibilities of calm,
That isolate the ne'er-do-well
From mansions he could own.

Silent Space

I linger at this spot of life,
As if a glimpse of memory,
Alike it stimulated some remembrance
Of now forgotten cask of treasured souvenir

That had recounted home.
It is a simple destiny of having been,
Clutching vintage fragments
That recount a cottage glen,

And forms delighting in belonging to each
Other there, some sire's embrace,
Some worn path at the ancient door
They stationed by in stark complacency.

It is a warmth that shrouds a cold,
A numb that stills some pain
At having lost the innocence of place
Where I could all belong.

So pile the tattered souvenirs
Upon this solitary nest of silent space,
That clutter round the isolation, forming like a frost
From some extinguished inner heat.

A Destiny

There is a destiny you cannot miss,
Though raging in a louding roar of life
That stimulate as roasting in a flame,
And consumate all wish of want and need.

You cannot slip beyond its reach,
Not pose, and preen a semblance of else,
And gaggle to the multitudes
As if you were a member of their flock,

And ply the gleaming course of power,
Amid its trinkets of glittered form
In acres of prosperity, as gentry
Suited in the latest wear.

It will find you, finally, its form
Like shadows on an x-ray in the lab,
Portend the fate which shall consume
Your so adult embrasure on the firmament.

Your hoard of being, shatter
Like heat upon a glass, the fragments
Sounding as the crack of doom
Only you can sense,

As if primal drum of ancient spawn
Sift through the ages of your consciousness,
And scorch the prim deceiving role
Upon the Broadway stage of prancing death.

There is a Mellowing

There is a mellowing in distance from the shire
Of once agos I trod as when
Some child, or fresh-formed youth
Whose happenstance was momentary joy.

How searing was experience,
So magnified, the captured images
Press permanent upon the madding self
In syllables and syntax down the destiny
Of now, I speak its semblance.

I smooth its ragged, misty form,
Now sharp intensity,
Though lensed to minute imaging
In scent, or color, or object, bring

As jewel, or link to majesty, or tick
Down in the mired brain, of clarity,
Of ghostly wholeness, of grasping satiation
In the present fading passage
Of darkening mortality.

Mary Herman

There is a place apart from time
We come to know,
Who have lost all we can to clocks,
And have no need of them to grow.

There is a place within the heart,
Bound in silver sterling bands,
That keeps a memory and hope,
And feeds on love of lands.

Where birds will sing and wild beast go,
Whose homes are built of moss and wood,
Through generations, safe, protected,
Living as they should.

For Mary holds the stewardship,
To keep them whole, and free,
Against the drums and teeming masses,
Who never let them be.

They are her legacy,
The trusting canine, feline eyes,
That are not turned away.
The land she has preserved forever,
Can never feel decay.

True value is not what one is,
But what one does, that lasts,
Beyond the birthdays of a lifetime,
The light of a lamp she lit, is cast.

(2010)

We Cannot Leash It

We cannot leash it with a stick,
Or drug, or damage done by sires,
Or self-recriminations of slipped fortune,
Or fame, or soulmates walking out.

All incidental, as the chitin crowd
Buzzing and scraping round us,
As we view skyward, toward sky lights,
Affixed by gravity and air.

It is the self we grow to be,
Around boulders on our face, on
Roiling maggots for our bed, it is
The thing that splits throught asphalt,

Blooms through orange pollution under
Cracked and warped boards, over broken glass,
Up out of staid drawing rooms, hot fudge
Wealth, and mindless power.

Controlled till death, the eyes within see it,
And look out at one last, horrified view to it,
Having missed a lifetime riding it
Up to those stars.

(2007)

There is a Touching

There is a touching that does not require flesh
To reach, not movement to embody,
Not grasping to attain, nor desire
To assume a greater hold

Could be upon the form by other means.
It is a silent thing.
It, unspent by force, unleased by sight,
Kindle searing light from dim,

Crisp from vague half seeing
Into bright, where from night
In darkness, pierce beam,
To quiet peering gleam.

This is the treasure of an instant,
Moment shot through in flight,
As passing spirit stimulation, flitter,
Where bitter crack, and glitter, seep like powdered gold.

(2008)

A Silent Destiny

There is a silent destiny,
Etheric chains, invisibles,
Like wires, guide unfeelingly,
Pull us to the blurred infinity

We call unknown, the mansion house
Where stand eternal station,
Where room enclose us,
Where we wait the pulsing moments through.

It is a fate we cannot move,
Though raging at a life,
Though noise consume us,
Though sharp activity define us,

We are moving steadily at pace,
We are enfolded into the home
That cannot be discarded as an age,
As fashion, as dull thought,

As controlling expectation divert us,
Seeming power define us,
As desire infect us, seep into us,
Fades quietly, as we assume our place.

(2007)

The Silence

There is a sound the silence makes,
No vestage of the ear could know,
No worldly form could recognize,
Not material in state.

It is the sounding of a soul,
That other, vapour'd thing,
That residue when all is taken,
When all is rotted through.

It is the child when we are old,
The joy apart at agony,
The home when have forgotten
Comfort possible, at memory.

It is the quieting, that stimulates,
The letting go of sense,
The wakening to such a whisper,
As angel wing could show.

(2016)

The Majesty of Life

This is the majesty of life,
The scrabbled, clawed to achieve,
Scraped to its summit majesty,
This is the achievement, this the throne.

Who would have thought had been so plain,
So silent, such expanse of still?
Who could have known such aiery peaks
Would be a solitary thing?

Though had been such a lonely climb,
The only peace was movement on,
The senses blind, the tramping endless,
Hungry fortitude for what was not in sight.

The battle all within, and out,
The sires disgust and hatred spawning indifference
As a universe to struggle in,
And come through, all passing by.

Who would have thought, the silence here,
The glacial isolation summit,
The steely, frozen paradise of success,
The long awaited home.

(2008)

Another Light

Un-night, other darkness,
Wet soft visioning, primal home,
Along your valley I become
A silent, ghostly thing, belonging.

It is not lack of light to be,
Not connected to the roar day,
Its dry, searing rush sounding
In motion it cannot stop.

It is another light, a silvered,
Gleaming spanse, my eyes are moon,
And vision in the still
Whose beast move soundlessly,

Plant wet with chalky mist
That is familiar to me,
Like a child long memory
Before the child.

Like ancient happening, still upon,
Still a place, like primal brain,
Whose memories of lizard things
Still become my sight.

(2016)

The Passing Day

It is passing day,
And at the pane I reach
To the silent light,
Its yellowed stillness
Just beyond my fingers.
From the window, gaze
Upon the massive scene
As if it were of canvas,
And laid on in paint,
Some formulation of nature's theme,
Now cast in some intensity of form,
I move to look upon.

It is the light, the lure to wake,
It is the thing all senses turn,
As some familiarity, from dark,
It is the setting to be at for move.
If I could reach the whole of it,
If I could stand at day,
I could be part of its embrace,
Its moment, at the crest of it,
Its happening at instants, daring
Some experience, some bold activity,
From what foundations are to memory.
I would be there, unlike this room,
The tug of secret darkness lessen
In that chalky scene of bright.

(2013)

You Came

Sweet, you came, but I was past the light,
My touch no longer at a fleshy form,
Though I had waited all my life for you,
Had stayed in faithful pose upon this room,
And lain in stillness in my bridal floss,
Had stationed at the door in gentle silence,
For your finding me.

I had smoothed the counterpane for two,
Had left so generous a berth for you,
My plaited hair encircled like some wreath
About my head, to cascade round you
At your fingertips, I waited there.

I drew back at a move, a light,
The curtain folding at myself,
At each passing thing beyond my window,
In the distance where I gazed,
In steady vigil, at my place.

There, like prayerful monk I stayed,
At my beads, my soul aflight
Into the dim candle essence, leaning for a sign,
A hope of you. There, came to be.
There, lived out my self.

The single reason of my breath, to supplicate
For you, to watch, my only purpose
Past the seasons, as the ages
Back and forth seemed to ply before me
Till my momentary light, so faded,
Now becomes a luminosity, unshaded.

(2013)

There is Another Face

There is another face within,
That has not shown itself to light,
Like tooth that never pushed above the suface,
Remains untouched within its silent dark.

It is the face we think we have,
When into light at morning stream,
A face that can express our wholeness,
That can be looked upon

As some cemented thing, some trinket in a box
That sires wore, some lode stone
That mountains knew at dawns of time,
Some still unchanging thing, like gem we fondle,

Whose sharp edge splay prismatic beams upon us,
Whose color does not fade and pale,
Whose familiarity like constant north, remain.
That is the face we move within.

That is the hope upon which hearts rely,
Which are not bloody pumps, but sugar forms
On glitter boxes, receptacle of loves,
Gauzed affection containers, sweet hopes holders.

That is the form we touch, our visage,
In remembering the fresh reflection in memory pool,
The dewy eyed enchantment at some dappled youth,
The magic mask, the invisible night reality.

(2010)

The Stark Invisibles

We are the stark invisibles,
The hollow, shattered, ghosting ones,
Who feed on darkness, shadowed blurring
On the edge of sight.

We are the silence between the sound,
Are what foundations stand upon,
And are not noticed in the whir of being,
Which vibrate into light.

We linger where the childhood passed on by,
Who calculate the memory of when,
Lit greenward to a scent of bower,
Stood as one, with everything.

(2016)

There is a Light

There is a light that does not warm,
It is not cast from furnace suns,
Does not illuminate a day,
Will not pierce the sensitivity of sight.

It is an inward beam, unknown by sense,
Unfelt, untouched, invisible
To life, as if it were an opposite
To all our being knows.

It does not register to life,
The breathing beast in movement
Spends its howling days so unaware,
So callous of its magic entity.

Yet it is what the firmament depends
Upon for molecules to bind,
For galaxies to hang suspended,
For what is life, to be.

It is reflected to us
As a mirror does the gaseous roar
Of bursting furnaces in dark,
That would blind to gaze into.

The globes of scorching, monster force,
That nourish only from a distance,
Only from a fraction of their possibility
Of power, of searing magnitude,

Yet it is only tapped at silence,
At dark, at letting go of possibility
Of individuality, of dereliction of memory,
Of future spent, at momentary presence,
Leaning into its endless beam.

(2013)

The Night

Throughout the night you have remained
Most fair between the two,
Who have lain upon this ancient bed,
Who have seen the darkness through.

Who had begun as seeming one,
As we slept on, but I awoke,
Through some necessity, or sound,
Regained a footing on the firmament,
And to some task, was bound.

Odd marching through the midnight realm,
From depths arose a stygian crew,
From blackest water broke,
Upon my landscape grew,
And meshed me in some horror brew,
While you slept on, just out of view.

Lain calm, unknowing of the demon froth,
The shackles round me lain,
And piercing with sharp, pointed fingers,
Into me probed like maggots, lain
Into me eating festered trails, in fetid pus,
Knit into my being, beside your silent form.

Your peaceful, pale somnambulence,
Your angel visage, cool in deep repose,
And silvered of the cresting moonlight,
As if some hoary vision at a mystic shrine,
Glistened in the colorless, transparent dark,
Shone, as beacon to the pilgrim wanderer.

(Continued)

I twisted in my coil of nightmare,
Aged recklessly at eons spent
In moments, as time, and place
Fractured in me, dissolving with me,
As you lie there.

And should the morning ever break,
Should we regain ourselves at day,
Would steadfast, firm activity, as early light,
Warm us, thaw the clotted, frosty night,
Return us unaware into a common,
Plodding, routine sight.

(2013)

Hungry Eyes

There is a depth that cannot fill,
Not level, not satiate, or satisfy.
It cannot cease its bold activity
To flood its hollowness with sight.

Hungry eyes, quick fury'd souls,
Where all desire flow, yet cannot pool,
All hope seek out, but does not recognize,
All agonies decipher, like rays,

Pierce into it, razors through it,
Earths of volumes into it,
Curving like prisim'd rays, reflecting
To it blooded rainbows

Of scarlet, shimmer'd brilliance
Blinding it, of substance weightless,
Formless, vapor'd things
That link in memory, second sight,

That sees, though ages multiply,
Clears, though sensibility decay,
Sees again its terror house
That does not dim, though eyes rot out.

(2016)

The Gilded Man

Huzzah for the gilded man,
Whose sinewed flank,
Like wildbeast sighted
At some mountain top,
Some jungle tangle
Where he prowl so soundlessly.

His sighting as a lodestone pull,
A lit flashed happenstance
Of sensuality no species could attain
As primal as this wanderer,

This glisten form, this grail
Whose nakedness convict our posing,
Choked in fabric, swaddling
Our hidden beast within.

Huzzah for the golden man,
Who strips society,
Which cracks sobriety, into
A dreamless, formless pulsing roar
Into immortal, gushing lust

Like fluids that we flow into,
Like darkened tides rise into,
Like senses shattering into a fracturing
Of self, of unity coming flow.

(2009)

For the Golden Man

Huzzah! Huzzah for the golden man!
The light, illusion piercer!
Golden man, who burns stiff calculation,
Who stills the racing mad.

Who is my pet, my dream come through,
My freedom from grey death,
Of anger, of formula activity,
Of convention, like raging terror

Yelled into me when I was helpless once,
And heard reverberations till at age.
And now it is the golden man,
It is the heart of bloody bliss.

The flowing river red, pierced red,
Hot red, its sticky substance roaring in me
In music old Orion sings.
Sing to the Golden Man!

(2009)

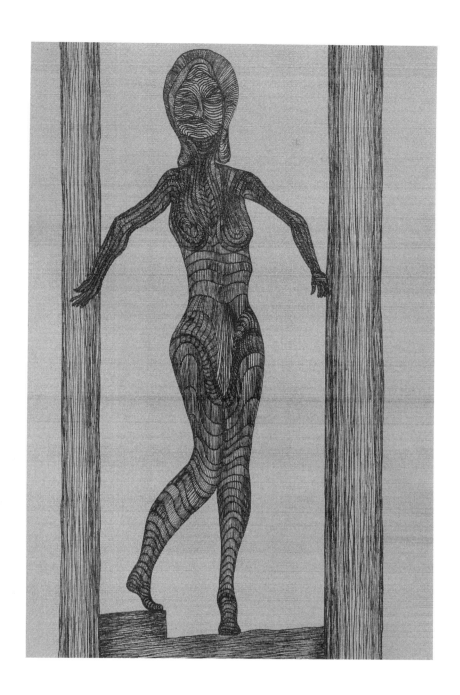

The Soul

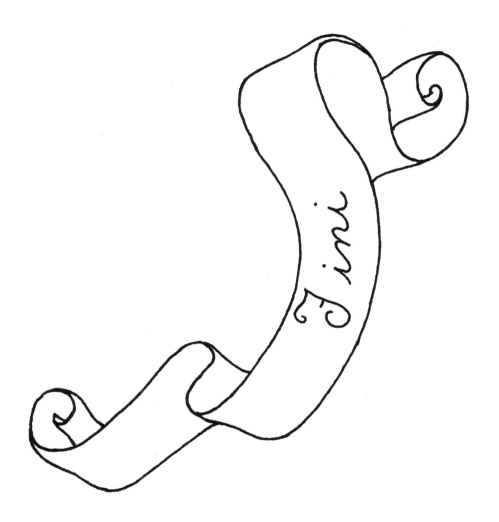

Poet and artist Michael Colby was born in Damariscotta, Maine, in 1949 and raised on the family farm outside Wiscasset. After high school, he attended the University of Maine at Orono. Following graduation, he hitchhiked across Canada to the West Coast and lived in a commune in Oakland, California. He obtained a teaching certification from Westminster College in Salt Lake City, Utah, where he began his teaching career. After meeting Don Graves, the men moved to Pennsylvania in 1979 looking for farmland. Influenced by the early Moravians who founded Bethlehem, they created their own spritiual community, the Hermitage, in the Mahantongo Valley of central Pennsylvania in 1988. Since retiring from teaching in 2007, the poet, now known as Zephram de Colebi, lives as a hermit and devotes himself to painting.

Palatino is a serif typeface designed
by Hermann Zapf (1918 - 2015).
It was introduced in 1948 by the Stempel
type foundry and adapted by the
Mergenthaler Linotype Company.

Made in the USA
Lexington, KY
29 September 2018